running a ring of spies

running a ring of

spies

spycraft and black operations in the real world of espionage

Jefferson Mack

Paladin Press • Boulder. Colorado

Also by Jefferson Mack:

The Safe House:
   Setting Up and Running Your Own Sanctuary

Underground Railroad:
   Practical Advice for Finding Passengers, Getting Them to Safety,
   and Staying One Step Ahead of the Tyrants

Running a Ring of Spies:
Spycraft and Black Operations in the Real World of Espionage
by Jefferson Mack

Copyright © 1996 by Jefferson Mack

ISBN 0-87364-902-8
Printed in the United States of America

Published by Paladin Press, a division of
Paladin Enterprises, Inc.,
Gunbarrel Tech Center
7077 Winchester Circle
Boulder, Colorado 80301 USA
+1.303.443.7250

Direct inquiries and/or orders to the above address.

PALADIN, PALADIN PRESS, and the "horse head" design
are trademarks belonging to Paladin Enterprises and
registered in United States Patent and Trademark Office.

Visit our Web site at www.paladin-press.com

Contents

Chapter One

The Easy Come Bar

The Easy Come bar wasn't the favorite spot of the thousands of GIs who took their R&R in Bangkok in 1969. Most Viet vets who spent time in Thailand will remember such places as the Hollywood, Thai Heaven, the Miami, the Green Dragon, and the California.

The Easy Come sat by itself, almost at the end of New Phetburi Road. For a GI bar in the R&R years, it was a small place, just a bar with six stools and four booths along one wall. I walked into the place one afternoon looking for possible spouts—the water taps of information in the business of foreign intelligence collection. I was working for one of a dozen different agencies in the alphabet soup of spies and diplomats that stalked the streets of Bangkok while war raged a few hundred miles to the east.

I sat in a booth, ordered a beer, and pretended for the moment that I didn't understand a word of Thai as three pretty girls slid into the booth with me, one beside me and two on the seat across from me. I fended off questions about where I was from and how many hours I had been in Bangkok while I slowly sipped a Singha beer. As the girls chattered on, I looked the place over while I listened to what they were telling each other whenever they spoke their own language.

I also took a good look at the Mamasan—the woman who managed the girls and took the money when a customer decided to buy a girl out for the evening. A tall, pretty Eurasian woman in her early thirties, the Mamasan sat behind the bar, watching with dark brown eyes everything that happened around her.

The Mamasan caught me looking at her and she smiled. I decided instantly that I was going to do my off-duty drinking in the Easy Come until I got to know her a whole lot better. I've always had a thing for smart, competent, strong, good-looking women. I left the girls sitting in the booth and walked over to the bar, carrying my bottle of Singha.

She looked up and focused on me as I asked her what her name was.

"Connie, with no last name," she told me and went back to working on the account book.

It took another four visits before she started talking enough to tell me her father had been a Dutchman who had lived in Thailand. He had taken Connie's Thai mother as his wife a few months before the Japanese captured and killed him during World War II. She had grown up poor and claimed she had opened the bar with money won in the Thai lottery.

I told her that I was a bright young American sociologist working with the Defense Advanced Research Projects Agency (DARPA) and was trying to discover how the Thai government could win the hearts and minds of its rural population before the Commies took over.

Maybe it was my suspicious nature, maybe it was because I was trying to learn everything possible about the spy business, but the more afternoons and evenings I sat in the Easy Come, sipping on a beer in a back booth and watching the parade of GIs on R&R and how well the girls handled them, the more what started as a tiny suspicion burning in the back of my mind became an open flame.

Counterintelligence wasn't my game in those days, so when I couldn't fight off the suspicion anymore, I took a lieutenant colonel working in Military Assistance Command, Thailand (MACTHAI) with one of the military intelligence services into the Easy Come for a beer one afternoon.

At first, George concluded there was no way Connie might be what I was afraid she was. Then, a couple of weeks later, an excited George walked into my office and told me he'd spotted Connie sitting with a group of American officers and their wives in the officers club at the Chao Praya hotel. Wondering what an R&R bar Mamasan was doing mixing with the American military elite, George asked one of those officers about the beautiful Thai woman and learned that Connie was a good friend of several military wives whom she had met in one of the Christian churches in Bangkok. None of the officers' wives appeared to have any idea that Connie was a successful R&R madam on New Phetburi Road.

The new information made George as suspicious about what Connie really was as I had been. Because he didn't think it wise that he go back into the Easy Come, he asked me to keep dropping in on Connie and playing the dumb government civilian hoping for an impossible love. That was fine with me, and after a while Connie and I got to be very good friends—to the point where I learned that while all those American wives thought Connie was a devout Christian, a large bronze statue of Buddha sat on a pedestal in one corner of her bedroom.

To this day George can't prove that Connie was doing what we both decided she had to be doing, but she was probably one of the most clever intelligence case officers who ever worked the business.

George never was sure for whom she was working, either. It could have been the Russians, Red Chinese, or North Koreans, or she might even have been an independent intelligence entrepreneur. But whoever she served, the gobs of information Connie's girls squeezed, fondled, and drew out of the parade of GIs who wandered into the Easy Come almost certainly went straight to Hanoi.

The dozen girls who worked in the Easy Come at any one

time were all a bit prettier, a lot more enthusiastic at love-making, and a whole lot smarter than the average girl just off the farm servicing GIs in the other places along the Phetburi strip. Connie's girls all spoke English, although sometimes heavily accented, but always well enough to ask questions and listen carefully while a guy fresh from a good orgasm bragged about what a great soldier he was.

The Easy Come girls were great actors who could sell an illusion of love as quickly as Houdini could slip out of hand-cuffs. Most of the time, a grunt who spent a night with one of Connie's girls didn't go looking for love anywhere else for the remaining days of his R&R. If he did want a change of vagi-nas, he went back to the Easy Come to find it. At least once a week, some soldier left town in desperate love with one of the Easy Come girls. Many of them kept writing the girl for weeks and months after their R&R. A few signed up for an extra tour in 'Nam just so they could get a 30-day leave and take it in Bangkok in the arms of one of Connie's girls.

It wasn't just vets from Vietnam who found the Easy Come. There were 40,000 U.S. airmen stationed in Thailand during those years, and a couple of thousand members of the other armed services worked out of the Joint United States Military Assistance Group (JUSMAG) and MACTHAI com-pound located near the U.S. Embassy on Wireless Road. Most of them considered a visit to the R&R bars the worst kind of slumming, but if they happened to stumble into the Easy Come, Connie made sure they found something a little extra special that brought them back time and again. I know of four different girls from the Easy Come who married Bangkok-based GIs during the years I tracked events in the bar, and at least half a dozen more who did tour-long shack-ups with U.S. military personnel. Every time a girl left to take up a full-time love situation, Connie would find another who fit the special personality of the Easy Come girls.

Probably 99 percent of the grunts who found the Easy Come didn't have much worth knowing locked up in their gonad-driven brains. But it was a dirt-cheap spy network with the U.S. GIs paying for most of the cost out of the money they had saved for months before getting a seat on an R&R flight. Connie was learning details about unit size and location, patrol operational techniques, ambush methods, unit morale problems, pending troop movements, beach defenses, river patrol routes, GI black market activities, and damn near anything else a GI might know about how America was fighting the war in Vietnam.

As for the guys stationed in Thailand, every secret known in the JUSMAG compound, including planned bombing targets in Laos, was at risk any time a soldier stepped into the Easy Come.

Connie had that knack for spotting a potential payoff that makes a case officer a master of the trade. Once in a while, one of the R&R customers would let it slip that he was working someplace important, like maybe the Military Assistance Command, Vietnam (MACV) compound in Saigon or a brigade headquarters up north. Marks like that went back to Vietnam and would soon thereafter meet a little Vietnamese hooch girl, or maybe even a European female employee with some international aid organization who seemed to know instinctively just exactly what the young man liked when it came to loving. None of the Americans had any reason to suspect that their sudden good luck in Saigon was directly tied to their R&R and the girls they left behind in Thailand.

Occasionally, someone would spill something big. George was sure that one of Connie's customers let slip the wrong bit of information back in Saigon to a French secretary working for a trading company, which resulted in a sapper attack that killed an Army of Vietnam (ARVN) two-star general in an explosion in a Saigon restaurant. I'll always be convinced that it was another of Connie's customers who blew the information about the surprise attack into Cambodia that allowed the Vietcong command structure to disappear before the troops got to the target.

Connie wasn't just working the R&R trade either. Playing her second role as the devout Christian Eurasian, she was doing all sorts of friendly things to help the U.S. military and embassy wives she met at church on Sunday survive the expatriate life in Bangkok. She arranged up-country trips to old temples, set up cultural nights where the Americans could watch Thai dancing, and even organized a Thai-American Buddhist study group.

She also helped the American ladies find household help. The Thai women whom Connie sent around to work as cooks, maids, and baby-sitters weren't quite as young and pretty as the girls sitting at the bar in the Easy Come, but they were bright, they spoke passable English, they worked hard, they treated the *farang* (American or European) kids with lots of love, and they didn't steal. Although none of the wives ever figured it out, or perhaps didn't want to admit it even to themselves, Connie's maids were also ready and willing to give the man of the house a quick taste of Thai love in the servants' quarters while his wife was off studying Thai culture with Connie.

George's military spooks never told the Thai government what they were sure Connie was doing. They didn't issue any warnings to the troops or warn the gaggle of military and embassy wives that their house servants were probably spying for the Communists.

Smart intelligence officers don't arrest, murder, or destroy the public image of good spies. They either use them or neutralize them, but they always try not to let the spies know they have been made. In the spy game, the devil you know is a thousand times better than the devil you don't know. Destroy a spy ring you know about and a new spy ring you know nothing about will soon be watching you.

After I alerted George about my suspicions of Connie and the Easy Come, he set up a section in his own organization that did nothing but monitor Connie and her activities. For the next two years, every GI who wandered into the Easy Come was photographed and identified by someone working for George. Those who were nothing but mud grunts went back to 'Nam, fought the war, and lived or died without ever suspecting how close they had come to a major spy ring. Those who did have access to information of potential intelligence value went back to Vietnam to find that new duties awaited them that kept their hands off classified documents and their asses much closer to real combat.

The same thing happened with the Bangkok officers' wives and their husbands who stepped into Connie's web. Most of them were never told the truth about Connie. The wives kept going on up-country trips and sitting through cultural education classes while their housemaids taught their husbands the subtle differences between Asian and American feminine anatomy.

A few guys did get sudden transfers, like one U.S. Air Force embassy attaché I personally knew who suddenly found himself flying combat missions out of Ubon while his family went back to the States.

Connie kept collecting a lot of information, some of it probably useful to those who received her product. What else was happening was that George's counterintelligence group starting feeding Connie's girls bits and pieces of false information. Some of the guys filtering into the Easy Come or encouraging their wives to take one of Connie's up-country trips knew exactly what they were doing—participating in what eventually became the single most effective disinformation campaign we had going in Southeast Asia until the time we pulled out of 'Nam.

For example, a rumor once suddenly flashed through the MACTHAI compound that entire companies in I Corps were unable to climb out of bed because of a new and virulent mutation of penicillin-resistant gonorrhea spreading through the troops. Within days, the officers' wives were all talking about it as they took one of Connie's up-country trips. A week later, a Vietcong battalion launched a series of surprise attacks in I Corps expecting to catch sick troops not fit for combat. They died on the wire in droves.

On another occasion, one of the U.S. Army's best snipers and his spotter took an R&R at the same time in Bangkok and went straight from their hotel to the Easy Come. Five days later, on the last night of a glorious time, the two of them got skunk drunk with two of Connie's girls and started talking to each other about their plans for taking out a key North Vietnamese battalion commander.

If the two men had really done what they talked about doing that night in Bangkok, they would have walked straight into an ambush. Instead, B-52s carpet-bombed the area, churning into hamburger two companies of the crack northern troops committed to the ambush.

This was an especially successful counterintelligence operation because George doubled Connie's entire spy ring without making any direct contact with a single member of the enemy network, a real coup in the intelligence game. While it is almost impossible to estimate the actual impact of the clever use of human resources in any spy operation, Connie unknowingly passed on enough false information that she probably did more for the U.S. war effort than many of the intelligence case officers working on our side.

Like all good things, it didn't last forever. Eventually, some general in Hanoi must have begun to suspect that the information supplied by Connie's spy ring was no longer as valuable as it had once been and that much of it not only proved to be inaccurate but it sometimes backfired. The more that happened, the less they could trust any information she produced for them.

In late 1971, I left Bangkok for a tour in another part of the world. The last time I dropped by to see Connie, she looked nervous, almost like she was frightened about something. I had gone in the Easy Come for a last good-bye and to tell her a cover story that I was quitting my government contract job and going home to get a law degree. Weeks before that, she had started hinting that maybe we should get a lot friendlier than we already were, which was pretty damn friendly.

Just before I got up from her bed to leave, she asked me why I didn't marry her and take her with me to wherever I was going. It was a serious offer, and I might have taken her up on it if there hadn't been a wall of lies between us that neither of us could ever break down.

I saw Connie once more in 1984 when I spotted her in a shopping center in Crystal City, Virginia, just a few miles from the Pentagon. She was hanging onto the sleeve of a guy I recognized as someone who had been assigned to MACTHAI back in the war years as an army major in the civilian contract office. Two kids just short of their teens were tagging along behind Mama and Daddy as they looked at new refrigerators.

It's not hard to figure out how Connie ended up in the United States, married with children. George's counterespionage operation was so highly classified that Connie's name would have never been put into any visa lookout files, nor the lookout files of other agencies. The guy she married had no idea what his wife had done during the war years or how his own government was using her without her knowing it.

As I stood watching her that day in Crystal City, I envied the guy just a bit. Then she turned and saw me standing there. She recognized me, but she neither smiled nor frowned. The man said something, and she turned, gave him a big smile, reached up, and kissed him on the cheek. When she finished the kiss, she turned and looked back at me for just a second, making sure I had seen the kiss. Then she turned and walked away, her arm locked with the arm of her American husband, a Norman Rockwell picture of the perfect cross-cultural marriage.

Like all good intelligence case officers, Connie could build a great illusion and make it seem so real that it really was. The son of a bitch looked as happy as any married man I've ever seen who was taking the family on a shopping trip.

Chapter Two

Spying Has One Purpose

nowing the enemy's defense plans, the secrets of a new weapon system, or the mental state of a political leader can cost or save thousands of lives, depending on who has the knowledge and how they put it to use.

Good spies can keep a government out of war, and incompetent spies can get a government into a war that can't be won. Governments don't just spy on enemies threatening war. The Cold War is over, but both the CIA and the KGB are still in business, and the intelligence case officers of dozens of different countries recruit and run rings of spies trying to uncover trade secrets, political plots, and military plans, as well as the plans of terrorist groups scattered around the world.

Governments also spy on their own citizens. The FBI tries to infiltrate the Mafia and dozens of other organized criminal groups, and the IRS not only collects and examines the financial documents of most major corporations as well as millions of private citizens, but also actively recruits and pays snitches willing to rat on their friends and employers for profit.

IT'S NOT JUST GOVERNMENTS
THAT HAVE REASON TO SPY

Almost all of us will at some time know something that will give us an advantage over someone else. Just as likely, we will sooner or later lose something dear and important to us because someone else found out something we thought only we knew about. Every one of us spies on someone else at one time or another.

- A mother may listen in on a teenage son's call to a girl-friend, hoping she will learn that the girl is not pregnant.
- A man will drive by a girlfriend's house to make sure she really is home with a cold.
- A wife will carefully examine the dirty clothes her husband brought back from a trip out of town, looking for signs of lipstick or strands of blond hair.
- An employee will sneak a look in the boss' file cabinet, trying to find out who will get the next promotion.
- A father will check out his daughter's boyfriend with a credit bureau.

ALMOST ANYONE CAN HAVE A
GOOD REASON TO RECRUIT SPIES

We can all face a situation in which someone has information we must have in order to survive or live well, and the only way we can get it is to steal it. Yet, most actions involved in stealing information—burglary, phone tapping, and bribery—are illegal acts with heavy punishments.

The safest way to steal information is to recruit someone who has access to the information who can steal it for us with little risk. Here are just a few examples of how ordinary people might recruit someone to spy on someone else.

- A professional gambler wants an extra edge so he can bet the odds that others set. He recruits as spies trainers, assistant coaches, secretaries, bus drivers, office managers, and even custodians and janitors who work for professional and college sports teams. His recruited spies provide bits and pieces of information on team morale, injuries, personality clashes, drug abuse, training practices, and any other information that might have an impact on the outcome of a game.

- The American Cancer Society recently discovered its private papers, dating to October 1979, in Philip Morris documents unveiled by *The New York Times* and accused the tobacco industry of spying on the society in the 1970s to learn how it planned to address the idea of safer cigarettes.

- Tom White is a successful lawyer who has spies working for him in three of the major insurance companies that handle many of the claims of injured parties Tom represents in court. As a result of the insider knowledge his spies provide, Tom almost never goes to court. When he does, he wins because he knows the strengths and weaknesses of the other side's case.

- Dan Cocker has made several million bucks in the stock market using insider information he collects from a half-dozen spies working in major investment firms.

WHAT GOVERNMENT
SECRETS SHOULD YOU KNOW?

Americans don't just have good reasons for spying on each other. Just as an intrusive government spies on its own citizens, so citizens often have good reason to spy on their government. The Mafia has been doing it for years.

Various action groups across the political spectrum, ranging from leftist radicals trying to discover CIA covert operations in Latin America to the new citizen militia groups worried about the Bureau of Alcohol, Tobacco and Firearms, are spying on government agencies.

Persons who are called investigative reporters are often

intelligence operatives trying to recruit government employees as spies so they can make money and fame by revealing the government's dirty secrets in headline stories.

Many of your fellow citizens as well as citizens in other countries have been spying on government officials for a long time. For instance:

- No one knows how many real estate speculators around the country have tapped into the secret planning meetings of county commissioners, state highway departments, and city and planning commissions.
- Any executive officer of any big corporation who isn't collecting daily information from a ring of spies working in the federal agencies that control and regulate every aspect of his business could be heading down a fast track to failure.
- One of the untold secrets of the business of lobbying Congress and state legislatures is that many lobbyists are more interested in intelligence than vote buying. U.S. congressmen and senators would be horrified if they knew how many people on their staffs are regularly passing information on to people representing businesses and industries that they are targeting for more restrictive regulation.
- Employees of the IRS, the Security Exchange Commission, the Patent Office, the Food and Drug Administration, the Federal Trade Commission, the Office of Safety and Health Administration, and on through the alphabet soup of bureaucracy all have tons of commercial information that they are supposed to keep secret. Yet each of those agencies has hundreds of unhappy, angry, indebt employees who can be recruited to provide such confidential information.
- A recent Associated Press report described how the Cali drug cartel has been spying on top government officials in Colombia. The operation gathered intelligence that when leaked to the press embarrassed the Colombian president and threatened the stability of the government.

WHO IS SPYING ON YOU?

Even if you live a life in which you can't imagine that you would ever have to spy on someone else, you may be the subject of someone else's spying. If you are the leader in a competitive industry, ever get involved in politics, take a public position on any divisive issue, or have a nice home and position in your community and people envy you, you know something that someone else can use against you—if he can find out what it is. It may be a manufacturing technique or process, a special recipe used in a restaurant you own, a guarded list of clients, an idea for a new invention, your credit card and PIN numbers, a secret love affair, a past you've overcome, a bit of extra income you don't report on your IRS form, or a vice that you keep hidden from the world.

If you want to protect your own secrets, you must know how successful spies operate so that you have some chance at spotting the person who you think is a loyal friend, a lover, a trusted employee, or a harmless, casual acquaintance, but who, in fact, is out to steal your secrets and give them to the person who will use them to do you the most harm.

Protecting yourself from those who would steal your secrets is as much a part of a personal defense strategy as arming yourself and guarding your fence lines.

Before we go any further, a note on semantics is in order. In an effort at brevity and clarity, I will use the pronouns *he* and *him* as nongender specific, rather than using the more awkward phrases *he or she* or *his or her*. This does not mean that females do not make excellent spies and case agents. In fact, some of the most dangerous spies and effective spy masters have been female, as the examples throughout this book make abundantly clear.

Chapter Three

The Basic
Principles of Spying

There are several different ways to steal secrets. Among the most effective of these means are the following three:

Observation and Surveillance: A spy sneaking into the enemy camp to count the sick and wounded, or hiding in the closet while others talk outside the door, is engaging in observation and surveillance. Modern covert surveillance includes using satellite photography, planting secret microphones, intercepting telephone calls, surreptitiously reading mail, and many other techniques.

The many technical advances in radar, sonar, spy satellites, long-distance and high-altitude photography, high-tech electronic intercepts, laser and parabolic mike audio collection, miniaturized microphones and video cameras, electronic signal interceptions, and computer-based deciphering of encrypted messages are all designed to improve methods of covert observation and surveillance. Modern national intelligence agencies spend the great majority of their budgets on high-tech surveillance.

Theft and Burglary: This is a frequent plot in spy movies and spy literature. The hero burglarizes an embassy, cracks the safe, takes picture of the secret documents, and then sneaks away with no one the wiser. Despite their popularity with authors of spy stories, burglary and theft are seldom used in the real world of spying. They are too high risk with too little chance of success. It was such an attempt at burglary that eventually brought down President Richard Nixon.

The Inside Spy: This means using a human being who has direct access to valuable secret knowledge to steal that knowledge. Some examples are the confidential informant in a drug gang who is under the control of DEA agents, the FBI plant driving a group of bombers around town while they plan to blow up the World Trade Center, the Soviet colonel passing on KGB secrets to a CIA contact, the U.S. Marine embassy guard entrapped into spying by a pretty girl he met in a Moscow cafe, or Aldrich (Rick) Ames, the CIA officer who made millions passing secrets to the Soviets while he drew his U.S. government paycheck. This is what intelligence officers are talking about when they use the word HUMINT when discussing intelligence collecting activities. (HUMINT stands for human intelligence, that is, intelligence collected by a human being rather than by capturing an electronic signal or taking pictures from a satellite.)

Despite the fact that human spies still operate in much the same way they have for the last several hundred years, the spy can often obtain information and intelligence that cannot be discovered by other means. The inside spy not only can gain access to documents and plans locked up in safes, he can provide information on what people are talking about in private, the personality strengths and weaknesses of enemy leaders, internal strife within an enemy organization, and the espionage techniques the enemy is using to steal secrets.

Sometimes the human spy can be an incredibly cheap source of intelligence, even though the product is extremely valuable. Such a spy may not even know that he is providing information to the enemy. That was the case with all those guys on R&R who walked into the Easy Come in Bangkok.

SPIES CAN DO MORE
THAN JUST STEAL SECRETS

Once an intelligence officer recruits a spy inside an enemy camp, he has someone at his command who is not only able to steal secrets but who can also engage in a variety of covert actions that will cause the enemy problems. A spy inside an enemy camp can engage in sabotage and spread rumors and lies that mislead the enemy and may even destroy the reputations of leaders. The temptation to use spies for more than stealing secrets is a problem every national intelligence agency faces. Every intelligence agency and those who hire the intelligence officers must always balance the demand for intelligence against the demands for using a spy for covert action.

Whereas this book will focus on the recruitment of spies with the intention of stealing secrets, anyone can use the same methods to recruit a spy who will destroy property, lose files, tell lies, spread rumors, play dirty tricks that demoralize the enemy, and engage in other destructive activities. Also, a spy who has been stealing secrets can often be redirected into sabotage.

SPY RECRUITMENT FACTS

Pick up any catalog of books on espionage and investigation techniques and you will find lots of titles explaining how to search through public records, even more titles describing surveillance techniques as well as the high-tech equipment available for surveillance and how to use it. There are also lots of books telling a potential spy how to pick locks and open safes. You can learn how to make bombs and dozens of different kinds of gadgets and tools that can be used for sabotage, how to tail a suspect, how to spot someone tailing you, and how to use computer encryption programs so you can send messages that no one except the person you send them to can read.

In all those instructions on how to spy, you will find almost nothing explaining how to recruit a spy who will report secret information from inside the enemy's camp.

The secrets of how to recruit spies are closely guarded by those who have learned how to use them. Such government intelligence agencies as the CIA, KGB, British MI6, and the Mossad go to incredible efforts to ensure that their methods of recruiting spies are not exposed to public view. Anyone who works for any of those agencies must sign a contract agreeing to never reveal the spycraft secrets learned while working as an intelligence collector.

The intelligence agencies of powerful world governments don't keep these trade secrets to themselves. The secrets of spy recruitment are anything but secret between agencies. The KGB knows everything the CIA knows about the different ways to recruit a spy. Nothing in this book is going to tell the KGB, Mossad, PLO, Mafia, drug cartels, or even the intelligence services of such countries as Peru, Bolivia, Cuba, and Uganda anything they don't already know.

Government intelligence agencies keep their recruiting techniques hidden from the public because they don't want the general population knowing how they recruit and use spies. This secrecy serves two purposes. First, it makes it easy for government agencies to recruit ordinary citizens as spies because such people don't spot the warning signals that they are being recruited. Second, the secrecy helps a government ensure that its citizens don't start spying on it and finding out just how incompetent, and sometimes criminal, it can be.

A SPY IS ALWAYS A TRAITOR

A spy steals information from people who trust him and to whom he owes loyalty and then gives or sells that valuable information to their enemies. Most people don't want to become traitors, and, just as important, those who would willingly become traitors are almost never in positions where they have access to secret information that an enemy might want to steal. Therefore, the intelligence collector must recruit spies who will do his work in such a way that 1) the recruits don't realize that they are spies, 2) he fools them into thinking they are not really doing anything so terrible, or 3) he traps them in a situation in which they have no choice but to give the enemy intelligence officer the information he demands.

This is the primary craft of the intelligence collector who must rely on human resources—the art of convincing people to commit treason against their country, their employer, their political associates, their friends, and even their loved ones.

Once a citizen understands the means of convincing people to spy on those who trust them, he has the tools he can use to learn the secrets of an intrusive government, the big corporation, the labor union, law firms, a criminal organization, or any other powerful group that wants to control his life and take his money and wealth. Just like the armed citizen is the primary defense against both the criminal and an unjust government, so too is the citizen who knows and understands the craft of recruiting spies prepared to defend himself against the criminal as well as a government intent on limiting the freedoms of its own citizens.

Politicians and bureaucrats don't want you to learn the secrets of spying for the same reasons they don't want you to keep your arms or your right to self-defense. The craft of spying can be as important a weapon in the defense of your freedom as any you can load and lock.

Despite the secrecy under which they are buried, the principles and secrets of spying are relatively simple to learn and practice. Anyone who wants to discover information someone else is holding can recruit and organize a ring of spies and put them to work ferreting out the required information. It need not be that expensive: a successful intelligence-collection operation may consist of as few as two or three people.

Chapter Four

Who Is a Spy
and Who Is Not

No employees of the CIA, KGB, MI6, Mossad, or any other international spy agency consider themselves spies. They will insist that they are loyal employees of their government, whose job it is to recruit spies. Often they work in the embassies of their country and are identified as diplomats or other government employees. Sometimes they work undercover as businessmen, journalists, students, or tourists, and sometimes they sneak into the country as *illegals*, that is, someone pretending to be a national or a legal resident of the target country.

Regardless of what cover they work under, they not only don't consider themselves to be spies, they almost always hold in contempt the people they recruit as spies and consider them to be low-life traitors to their own country and culture.

Intelligence officers who recruit and run spies to spy for them are called *case officers,* or *case agents.* The *spy*, or the *agent*, as he is called in more polite talk, is the traitor who sells or gives away secrets he has been entrusted to keep safe. This book explains how the case officer does his work and how any ordinary citizen can practice the same skills in the private collection of intelligence. The case officer is the keystone of all HUMINT intelligence-collection operations. Every ring of spies has a case officer who recruited each spy and who controls and manages the activities of each link in the ring.

THE ATTRIBUTES OF A CASE OFFICER

In his book *The Craft of Intelligence*, Allen Dulles listed the personal attributes of a good case officer as someone who possessess the following characteristics:

- is perceptive about people
- works with others under difficult conditions
- is able to distinguish between fact and fiction
- is able to distinguish between the essentials and the non-essentials
- possesses inquisitiveness
- pays attention to detail
- has good oral communication skills
- knows when to keep his mouth shut
- understands other points of view, and
- is highly motivated and does not depend on public recognition

Dulles also claimed that he preferred to recruit the good, honest citizen and train him to be an intelligence officer rather than to seek out people who are naturally devious, conspiratorial, or wily.

If Dulles actually believed that, it explains why U.S. intelligence has so often failed, especially in the recruitment of human resources. "Boy Scouts" who respect and obey the rules of honesty, trustworthiness, loyalty, and friendship don't do well as case officers, who necessarily have to be devious, conspiratorial, and dishonest.

My experience with U.S. covert intelligence officers who did produce good intelligence by recruiting spies successfully is that they were indeed naturally devious and that they took to the career they chose like wolves to the hunt. They considered the ability to deceive to be a major part of a game they enjoyed playing, and they developed great pride in their abilities to deceive.

DIFFERENT WAYS TO FIND A SPY

The person who wants to recruit and manage a ring of spies has several different types of personalities he might recruit to do the dirty work of spying. Each different type becomes a spy for a variety of different reasons and emotional motivations.

The Inadvertent Spy

These are people like all those GIs who walked into the Easy Come while on R&R in Bangkok. They don't deliberately become spies, but instead give away secrets without knowing what they are doing. They are men and women with loose lips, bad judgment, and careless security attitudes, who talk business with colleagues in bars and restaurants and who brag about their work to their lovers, their friends, and sometimes to perfect strangers. They are the sources of information that intelligence officers like most of all. They cost little or nothing to cultivate, and they present few risks to the case officer.

For the private citizen who is trying to get information on a competitor, a local government agency, a businessman with whom he is having a dispute, or a bad neighbor or personal enemy, the inadvertent spy can often be the only source one needs to cultivate. The trick is to figure out how to get such a person talking about what he knows without letting him guess that he is making a big mistake that may cost dearly.

The Defector as a Spy

Much of the intelligence information that the United States collected from human resources during the Cold War came from people who fled the Soviet Union or one of the other communist countries. Most were anxious to share any secrets they brought out with them in exchange for new identities and a chance to live in suburban America. Although most refugees fleeing the communist paradises had little or no intelligence information, occasionally a defector would come from the KGB, the Soviet military, or some important ministry. That didn't happen all that often, however, because though life in the Soviet Union was hard and brutal, those who successfully built careers in the government bureaucracy or military command structure enjoyed a living standard far above that of most citizens.

When defections from the upper ranks did occur, the intelligence usually had value for a limited time. The Soviet security apparatus, knowing that the defector had fled to the West, would immediately initiate a damage-control operation by changing code books, withdrawing case agents and spies the defector might know about, and sometimes even moving critical plants and weapons locations.

A good case officer can encourage someone to defect by using many of the same techniques used to recruit spies. However, it makes much more sense to recruit a spy than to encourage someone to defect. A spy will continue to provide intelligence for many years; a defector is a one-time intelligence source.

High-ranking Soviet defectors would sometimes contact Western intelligence officers prior to their defection and attempt to make a deal for resettlement in return for intelligence information. When that happened, Western intelligence officers would try to talk the potential defector into remaining in place for a few months or years and serving as a spy. There is no evidence that many potential defectors bought into such a deal.

The Soviets benefited from very few defectors from the Western ranks. In most cases in which Western citizens with intelligence information defected, they were long-time spies such as Kim Philby, who fled to avoid capture after being exposed as a spy.

The Walk-In Spy

People sometimes walk in and volunteer to spy. That's what John Walker, a U.S. Navy petty officer working as a code clerk, did when he walked into the Soviet Embassy in Washington, D.C., carrying with him a collection of stolen documents as evidence of what he could provide. Walker was motivated purely by a desire to make money, and he eventually proved to be one of the most valuable spies the KGB ever ran.

CIA agent Rick Ames did the same thing, although he didn't have to walk into the Soviet Embassy. His job put him directly in contact with Soviet intelligence officers, and all he had to do was drop a few hints that he was looking for new sources of income. Ames did his native country even more damage than Walker.

One reason why so few Americans ever defected to the Soviets is that the American who was willing to sell out his country could live very well by staying in place for years, enjoying the advantages all of us in this country enjoy, plus the extra luxuries paid for with the money they earned as traitors.

Despite the fact that walk-ins can be very valuable, most covert intelligence agencies don't trust them. There is always the suspicion that the walk-in might be a plant (that is, a deliberate attempt by the enemy to spread disinformation and fake intelligence) or a total fraud—someone trying to sell intelligence he doesn't have and can't get.

Everyone knows that the CIA, KGB, MI6, and every other intelligence agency around the world will pay good money for secret intelligence. A surprising number of people think they can cash in on that by pretending to have access to secrets when they don't. Sometimes fraudulent walk-ins are psychotics who believe they are getting secret information from psychic vibrations, foreign spaceships, or a tooth filling that picks up radio waves from distant countries. More often, the frauds are deliberate crooks hoping to make an easy buck. If they also happen to hold real government jobs, they may actually collect money for a while before they are found out.

The stories that such frauds try to sell as intelligence information often follow the headlines. For years after the fall of Vietnam, every U.S. Embassy in Southeast Asia saw a string of people walking in and claiming they had intelligence on U.S. GIs still missing in action. The more clever frauds would tell complicated stories, carry detailed maps, and sometimes even photos of supposed prisoners who were still alive. All of those frauds shared one common thread: they claimed that there was one piece still missing, but that they could find that piece if they only had a bit of money—say, a million dollars or so—to pay off the right prison guard, Vietnamese military officer, local merchant, or other source.

So many walk-ins do indeed prove to be either frauds or persons deliberately attempting to spread disinformation that it's easy to understand why intelligence officers have been known to dismiss legitimate walk-ins as frauds.

One of the most productive spies the CIA ever ran inside the Soviet Union was Oleg Vladimirovich Penkovsky, a highly placed Soviet military officer who was apparently motivated by a political conviction that he was preventing a disastrous world war by passing on secret defense information to the West. Yet the first time Penkovsky approached the Americans, the CIA rejected his offer to spy because it was convinced that he was a Soviet plant trying to spread disinformation. It was only after British MI6 took up Penkovsky's offer and started verifying what he was providing that the Americans realized they had made a serious mistake in not grabbing him the first time he tried to volunteer. Penkovsky provided a huge amount of information for the next several years. Eventually the KGB caught on, probably because of their own intelligence penetrations of the CIA and British intelligence, and Penkovsky was arrested, tried, and executed.

Walk-ins don't happen just at the international political level. Just about anyone with a grudge against a commercial company, government agency, or political organization with which he works can decide to take revenge by talking to someone willing to pay good money for good information.

The Planted Spy

One way for an intelligence agency to get a spy in the right place is to have someone seek employment with the government, business, or agency that the intelligence officer wants to spy on. This is called *insertion, placement,* or *going undercover.* This should not be confused with the *illegal* case officer, who is a case officer who sneaks into a country with a false identity with the intention of recruiting spies once he is there.

Although it is a popular fiction plot, national spy agencies almost never attempt to plant one of their own employees inside a foreign government. The CIA would not, for example, attempt to infiltrate a trained CIA intelligence officer into Cuba with the expectation that he would seek employment with the Cuban Ministry of Defense by using a false identity. The risks of such an operation are too great, and the difficulties of establishing a credible cover are almost insurmountable. Even if the effort succeeded, the spy might have to remain in place for years, living a constant lie, before he ever won the promotions necessary to give him access to secrets that would be worth stealing. Also, there is always a chance that as the person stayed in place, he would make friends and eventually grow so close to those with whom he worked that he would refuse to spy, or worse, that he would become a double agent.

Such law enforcement agencies as the DEA and the FBI will sometimes insert a spy into some criminal organization. Although a police officer may go undercover, it will almost always be for a short period of time, generally no more than a few days. Instead, police agencies will usually try to plant a spy inside a criminal organization by making a deal with a criminal they have caught, promising him a lesser sentence if he can produce evidence on a suspected criminal organization by working as a member of the gang.

It is almost always easier to recruit someone who is already in place than it is to insert a spy as a new employee. Anyone intending to engage in a bit of domestic spying should first attempt to recruit a spy in place and should only consider the possibility of planting a spy when recruitment efforts have proved to be impractical or impossible.

The Recruited Spy

If an intelligence officer can find no one with loose lips nor anyone wants to defect to his side, and he knows that planting a spy is unlikely to work, then his only option is to recruit someone who is already working for the government agency, business, or political organization he wants to spy on. Such a person will probably have no intention of spying on those who trust him and would immediately reject an unsolicited offer that he spy for money. Therefore, the case officer will have to figure out a way to trick, bribe, or blackmail such a person into agreeing to become a spy.

The Doubled Spy

The final way to find a spy is to catch someone spying on you. As we learned in the first chapter, most spies aren't shot when they are caught; they are doubled. Either they are used without knowing they are being used—like what happened to Connie and her girls—or they are forced to cooperate. Those who catch the spy give him a choice of either being shot, spending a major portion of his life in prison, or working for the people he has been spying on while pretending to still be loyal to those who recruited him as a spy.

Generally, like in Connie's case, doubled spies are used to pass fake intelligence to the enemy, hopefully intelligence that will convince the enemy that one is stronger, better prepared militarily, and readier to fight than the enemy previously estimated. Doubled spies can also provide information on the enemy's intelligence methods. They can explain how they were recruited, how they made drops, how they were handled, who their handlers were, and all the other details of running spies. The spy who is caught, and then doubled, will also have to come clean about what damage he has already done. He will have to provide all the details on what kind of intelligence information he passed on to the people he was spying for.

This kind of information is so important that even when a spy can't be doubled, it still pays to get him to talk. That's why intelligence agencies are always willing to plea bargain when they catch one of their own spying for the enemy.

DIFFERENT KINDS OF AGENTS RECRUITED BY CASE OFFICERS

Depending on the type of intelligence operation he is running, a good case officer may recruit three different types of agents: primary, access, and support. All of them will be traitors in that they will be working for the enemy while pretending to remain loyal to their country, employer, political group, or family.

A *primary agent* is someone who is working in a position in a government, military force, or political group where he has direct access to secret documents, the conversations of senior officers, or, better still, someone who directly participates in policy-making or operational activities.

A primary agent can also be a mistress, secretary, driver, messenger, or anyone else who has access to documents, communications, and personnel who deal with secret information. The girls at the Easy Come were working as primary agents for Connie, their case officer.

An *access agent* is a recruit who does not have any direct access to useful intelligence or any personal relation to such people, but who may know someone who does. An access agent may also have access to places where potential primary agents work or play. The access agent can then report on people who might be recruited as primary agents and help arrange for the case officer to make an approach. An access agent may even do some recruiting under the close supervision of the case officer.

Access agents can also be used to place hidden microphones, cameras, and other technical surveillance devices. For example, a case officer might recruit a janitor working in an embassy and have him plant a microphone in the ambassador's office while cleaning it out.

A *support agent* is also recruited by a case officer, who will usually have a number of these agents. A support agent performs services for the case officer such as doing surveillance duty, managing safe houses, clipping news stories, renting cars, making and picking up drops, purchasing supplies, and so on. Often they are openly employed by government intelligence agencies and report to work at the case officer's embassy. Most case officers will employ more support agents than actual spies. The same basic techniques are used for recruiting each kind of agent.

A ring of spies is not a sports team in which each player knows how he relates to every other player on the team. In most cases, the spies in a ring of spies won't know who the other spies are. They operate under the security principle of compartmentalization, which requires that each player in a spy ring be given only that information that he needs to know to do his job.

The reasons for this are obvious. First, if one spy is identified (compromised), the enemy cannot use him to identify other spies or verify that they exist. Indeed, the best scenario is one in which the captured spy believes he is the only person spying on the operation. Second, the case officer can use each one of his spies to verify information collected from his other spies.

An intelligence agency like the CIA can achieve even more effective compartmentalization by using different case officers to recruit and run different spies working within the same target organization.

Sometimes it is necessary to have two or more recruited

spies working together in what is usually called a cell. The primary agent might be reporting to an access agent to pass on the information to the case officer, while also depending on a service agent to develop exposed camera film. The Soviets made very effective use of such a cell structure in the early years of the Cold War. Whittaker Chambers and Alger Hiss were members of one such cell within the U.S. Department of State. Many intelligence experts believe that other such cells existed but were never discovered. Because of Soviet compartmentalization, Chambers had no information on the existence of such cells.

Even though the spies or the cells of spies will not know about each other, the case officer must manage each individual in the ring so that the work of each spy complements the work of the others.

WHAT THE GOVERNMENT CAN DO, ANYONE CAN DO

Anyone who knows the techniques that case officers working for the CIA, KGB, MI6, and Mossad use to recruit spies can use those same techniques to operate an intelligence-collection operation against any business, government agency, political organization, or individual.

- First, you must determine what information it is that you must have, who probably has it, and who has access to those who have the information.
- Second, you must determine what the best way of getting that information is, what it will cost to get such information, what the chances are of getting caught in the process, and what difference having the information might make in success or failure.
- Third, you must make a plan for getting the information and then implement that plan.
- Fourth, if you are successful, you must determine whether or not the stolen information is true.

- Finally, after concluding that the information is valid, you must act on it, even if you must change your mind about reality (the truth of the situation, regardless of whether it is what you want to hear, or not).

Just as the Mossad is much smaller than the KGB, the private citizen working as a private intelligence officer can down-size his effort to meet the limitations of his needs, budget, and time. Just one person may fill all the intelligence functions involved in a lawsuit, a small-business labor problem, a dispute with some local tax or licensing official, or an argument with a neighbor over a fence line, neighborhood nuisance, or bit of vandalism.

Even so, the private citizen who sets out to recruit and run a ring of spies still faces the same problem confronting every intelligence case officer: how does he convince someone to turn traitor and start spying on people who trust him?

Chapter Five

The Making of a Traitor

W hy would anyone turn traitor? How does an intelligence case officer make it happen? There are only four basic ways to get someone to do what you want them to do: 1) offer mutual cooperation to reach a common goal, 2) suggest a bargained exchange, 3) use fraud, and 4) use force.

- *Mutual cooperation* occurs when two or more people want the same thing and agree to work together to achieve that goal. A whole town turns out to fight a fire and save the town. A man and a woman marry and raise children together. A band of revolutionaries risk life, limb, and fortune because they all want a new form of government.
- The *bargained exchange* is the basis of the free market. It is how we get strangers to do something we want or give us something we need. We do it by agreeing to give them something we have that they want. As Adam Smith pointed out, the baker cares not a whit for my happiness, but he

supplies me with bread in return for the money I pay him.

- *Fraud* occurs when one person convinces another person to do something with a false promise that he will get something he wants in return. A politician promises the voter good government and low taxes when he intends to use government for his own enrichment and expects to raise taxes to make that possible. A television evangelist promises eternal life and the love of God to all who will send him money, even though he knows he cannot guarantee either. What we call manipulation is almost always fraud. We manipulate someone into doing our bidding by convincing him that he will get some reward that we can't deliver.
- With *force*, we threaten to injure, kill, or physically restrain someone unless he does exactly what we want him to do. His life or his money! Pay his taxes or go to jail! Sign the treaty or go to war!

Often, this process of winning cooperation takes place with little or no thought. Two men agree to go fishing and help each other through the day because they both want to catch as many fish as possible, or maybe they just want the pleasure of each other's company. We walk into the drugstore, pick up a package of razor blades, and take it to the cash register to pay for it. We drive the speed limit that is posted and pay our taxes without complaint.

Sometimes, someone must first convince us that it is in our own best interest to participate in a deal by selling us on the benefits we will receive by using a certain kind of soap, giving to a charity, or enlisting to fight in a war. Salesmanship thus becomes an integral part of the equation. A good sales technique can be merely educational, but most often it includes a large dose of fraud and manipulation.

The person who wants to recruit a spy must convince the potential recruit that it is in his own best interest to spy on those who trust him.

The Spy Who Believes in the Cause

The easiest spy to recruit is one who wants what he thinks his spying will produce. Julius and Ethyl Rosenberg and Kim Philby became Soviet spies because they wanted a Socialist world, and they thought that spying for the Soviets was the best way to get it. Soviet citizens sometimes became spies for the United States because they saw the failures of communism within their own society and the human misery it produced, or they feared that the Soviet leaders were risking a disastrous nuclear war.

Usually, when someone is driven to treason by ideology, he still loves his country but believes that the country's leaders have failed the nation and are leading the society down the road to ruin. Such people rationalize treason by insisting that they are not betraying their nation, their birthright, or their culture, but instead are opposing the evil people who have taken control of the government.

Playing on this natural human tendency, U.S. intelligence officers assigned to recruit Soviet agents would never say anything negative about Russia, the culture, or the people, but would instead try to separate the Communist Party apparatus from the Russian nation. They acted toward their recruits as though they were not recruiting traitors, but rather patriots willing to risk all by opposing the criminals who had taken control of the Motherland.

Spies for Pay

"Give me the secrets I want to know and I'll make you a rich man." Many spies do it for the money. This is the easiest motivation to understand and, indeed, to put to use. We don't like to admit it, but greed drives every human being. Almost everyone has a price, and once an intelligence officer knows the price of any individual, the process of recruiting is reduced to bargaining the exchange: how much will it cost me for each secret you steal?

Traditionally, intelligence officers, especially those who

have previously worked with true believers, have distrusted the spy motivated by greed. A greedy person is often difficult to control and manipulate because his loyalties only extend to the next higher offer for his services. Yet in the modern world, money has played an increasingly important role in the recruitment of spies. This has been especially true in the recruitment of Americans willing to spy for the "Communist bloc" countries. Aldrich Ames, John Walker, and FBI agent Richard Miller were all in it for the money.

Once the KGB and its allies learned how easy it was to buy some Americans, their recruitment efforts in the last years of the Cold War focused increasingly on those most likely to be enticed by financial reward—young, low-paid personnel such as code clerks, secretaries, and similar government employees, who did not belong to the privileged class of the upper-echelon bureaucrat.

Crass spies willing to turn traitor for a profit are easy to recruit, once they have been identified. They are often walk-ins. In other cases, a potential recruit may be initially hesitant to turn traitor for money, and the case officer will first have to do a selling job. Like any good salesman, he will have to psychologically manipulate the prospect to overcome initial resistance to the idea of selling out for money.

WHAT TO DO WHEN YOU CAN'T FIND A TRUE BELIEVER OR A GREEDY BASTARD

Most of the time, an intelligence case officer is not going to find either a true believer or someone anxious to make money who has access to the secrets the case officer wants. Most people believe in the cause or the company for which they work. They not only believe in it, they think of themselves as the kind of people who cannot be bought, no matter how much money might be offered.

Convincing a Recruit That He Is Doing the Right Thing

This means that the case officer will have to use fraud and manipulation in order to recruit the great majority of spies who have access to the wanted secrets. The case officer must make the potential recruit believe that his own personal interests will be best served if he becomes a traitor.

One way to do this is to convince the recruit that the case officer is actually on his side; that is, that they both share the same ideals and goals. Another way is to manipulate the recruit into believing that by spying, he will earn rewards that are rightfully his and, therefore, justify his turning traitor.

To do this the case officer uses the same techniques a good salesman uses to convince someone to buy an insurance policy that doesn't make good economic sense or a car much too expensive for his budget. In the case of the car, the salesman might first suggest that the customer really deserves such a fancy piece of iron and then manipulate him into concluding that he can handle the payments.

In convincing a potential recruit to spy, the case officer, like the car salesman, must play to the target's emotional needs, greed, and fears. The emotional needs can be based in ideology or personal desires, which can include revenge, anger, idealism, loneliness, or recognition by someone, even an enemy.

Anger

A common emotion that motivates many a person to turn traitor is anger at how his government, employer, or associates have treated him. The potential traitor may feel cheated because he has been passed over for promotion, unjustly accused of something, or simply ignored. The anger may be directed against either an individual, perhaps a supervisor, or the entire system. Other emotions that may inspire someone to turn traitor can range from despair or depression to a simple desire to be loved and appreciated.

There are always people who believe that their leaders are

misguided and incompetent or that they are unappreciated by bosses and co-workers and have been treated unfairly, causing them to lose their faith in the goals of the organization, but they don't know what to do next. However, even though the subject may have lots of anger bubbling up inside him, he will probably not be thinking about turning traitor when first approached by a case officer. It is up to the recruiter to figure out how to manipulate that anger or other emotion in a way that will convince the subject that turning traitor is the best way to get his revenge or make the world right again.

Sex

Sexual desire is an emotion on which intelligence case officers often play. Sometimes the potential recruit is deliberately baited with a potential lover. Once love breaks out, the case officer can make it appear that the lover is in serious trouble, which can only be resolved if the target turns traitor. This was the case with U.S. Marine Clayton Lonetree, who was a security guard in the Soviet Union in the 1980s and was caught spying for sex, court-martialed, and imprisoned.

Fear

Fear is another powerful force that can be used to manipulate people into doing what they don't want to do. Case officers can blackmail some people into spying. "Do me this favor, and I won't tell that you are a homosexual." Intelligence agencies are especially interested in potential recruits with such secret vices as drug addiction, sexual perversion, a gambling habit, or any past history they would prefer not be exposed. Also, once a person has been recruited by manipulating either his emotions or his greed, the case officer may use blackmail as a means of ensuring that the traitor remains loyal to his new master.

Using Force as Persuasion

People can be forced to spy. It's a technique that law

enforcement agencies use all the time. They arrest a low-level drug dealer, prostitute, bookie, or some other petty criminal, then they threaten to put him in jail for many years unless he agrees to spy on more important criminals.

The Gestapo, the KGB, and other police intelligence agencies often used the threat of violence to recruit spies, if not by direct threats to the potential spy then his family: "Remember, you have a wife and a child still living in the old country."

Criminal organizations in the United States and other countries also use threats of violence to recruit spies. Often the threat will be sweetened with some kind of financial reward. It's what the Mafia calls "an offer you can't refuse."

Although such threats do work with criminals and sometimes with people who have family living in police states, they seldom succeed in the international spy game or in cases of private spying. You can never predict how someone else will respond to the threat of violence, but many will choose to fight back. They will go to the police or their security officer. The risks of exposure for threatening violence are simply too great.

The smart case officer who needs a spy, and who can't find someone willing to sell out for payment, very probably won't even consider the idea of threatening to commit violence. Instead, he will look for someone he can manipulate into spying by playing on his emotions to the point where the target slips into spying without realizing what is happening.

REAL LIFE IS ALWAYS COMPLICATED

Most successful recruitments involve a combination of inducements and threats, which play on several different motives that might be driving the person targeted for recruitment. The potential recruit could be a closet homosexual who recently lost a promotion for reasons that had nothing to do with his sexual choices, who is deep in debt, and who just had a long-time lover drop him.

The clever case officer will use each of these emotional distresses to manipulate the target into turning traitor. He might first find a new lover for the target, have the lover help build the hate toward the company that refused to promote the target, add a touch of blackmail, and then throw in an offer of easy money to clinch the deal.

LEARNING THROUGH CASE STUDIES

Most government intelligence-collection agencies use the case-study methodology in training programs for their case officers. Like most of the case studies in this book, the following case is taken from a real-life situation, but background information and names have been changed for all the usual reasons. The serious student who is trying to learn the art and science of spying should not spend a lot of time attempting to figure out whether any case study is the real story behind the headlines, but instead should look for what the example teaches about espionage.

Knowing How the Game Is Played
Doesn't Make Someone Immune

Ted Brennan joined the CIA right out of college in the early 1960s, convinced that he was taking up a macho career that would be exciting and rewarding at the same time he helped protect America from the communist conspiracy. Things went well at first, but over the years he became increasingly disillusioned with the nitty-gritty deception that makes up the daily grind of the intelligence case officer working in a foreign country. The promotions didn't come as fast as he expected, and he had several personality clashes with senior officers whom he considered incompetent dolts anxious to report whatever the national political leadership wanted to hear, no matter what the truth might be.

The job also took a toll on his personal life. His wife, Millie, grew tired of the problems and isolation of living in foreign countries and frequently fought with him over the long hours of unpaid overtime that Ted put in. Eventually they divorced, and Millie took the children back home to Indiana. Ted found himself paying alimony and child support for three children he almost never saw while his ex-wife went back to college. Ted was left with no money for the simple luxuries bachelor men are supposed to enjoy. When a mutual-fund investment he had purchased on the advice of a U.S. businessman turned sour, he added to his list of miseries an anger at the entire American corporate world.

Then, while on an assignment in Buenos Aires, he met Linda, a Peruvian who was working in Buenos Aires with an international nongovernmental charitable organization. Linda brought some excitement back into Ted's life, not just on a sexual plane, but intellectually as well. While Ted had gone through college as a jock with little interest in political theory, Linda introduced him to books on international politics and a world of ideas they discussed with a collection of Argentine and expatriate intellectuals living in Buenos Aires.

Totally disenchanted with his career and anxious to marry Linda, Ted began looking for new employment outside of government. He discovered that such opportunities were practically nonexistent for disenchanted CIA case officer in midcareer. Feeling trapped and frustrated by the system, Ted found himself increasingly fascinated with the socialist philosophy that Linda and her friends argued as solutions for everything Ted saw going wrong with his personal piece of the world.

The one thing going right was that Linda held a U.S. immigrant green card and would soon be eligible to apply for U.S. citizenship, a necessary step before Ted could marry her and still keep his security clearance. Three weeks before she was to take that step, a man handed Ted an envelope on a busy street in Buenos Aires, then jumped into a waiting car and sped away. Ted opened the envelope to find documentary evidence that Linda, while a student in Peru, had belonged to a Peruvian political group associated with the Sendero Luminoso or "Shining Path," the Maoist narcoterrorist insurgency in Peru with deep ties to the coca trade and a long history of graphic terrorism. The package contained no messages or any threat of blackmail, but Ted was sure that would soon come.

Ted assumed that whoever had passed on the information intended to blackmail him, probably in an effort to enlist him as a spy. Nevertheless, instead of immediately going to his security officer, he told Linda about the package. She admitted that she had belonged to the political organization for a short period of time several years earlier but insisted that she had dropped out once she discovered the connection to the violent Sendero Luminoso.

Although Ted believed Linda's claims of innocence of any intentional involvement with violent revolutionary activities, he also knew that if the CIA security personnel learned of the information, they would never approve of his marriage to a person with such a history. Indeed, even continuing to date Linda would be a serious breach of security that would cost Ted his security clearance. Ted also worried that his own security people might have passed him the documentation as some kind of test to see if he would handle the revelations according to regulation.

Linda tearfully announced that the only course of action was for them to immediately stop seeing each other. She insisted that Ted should go straight to his security officer, report the incident, and give the embassy the evidence of Linda's past political activities. That would save Ted's career, but the exposure of Linda's past political indiscretions would cost Linda her job and make her ineligible for U.S. citizenship. Unemployed and unable to travel to the United States, she would have no choice but to return to Peru where she might face charges of sedition by the Peruvian government.

Ted angrily replied that he would instead resign immediately. They could then get married as soon as possible and start over in some other country. Linda pointed out that neither would have a job or any prospects for finding employment. Linda would still have to go back to Lima, and it would take months or even years for Ted to find some kind of work that would allow him to support Linda in a country other than the United States.

As they discussed the problem through the night with time out for a couple of intense sessions of lovemaking, Ted became more and more vociferous in his disdain for his career with the government. He repeatedly insisted that he would do anything to protect their love and keep Linda safe from harm. Near dawn, Linda tearfully proposed one possible solution, provided Ted really was convinced that the CIA was not the protector of freedom that Ted had once thought it to be. Ted agreed immediately to meet with "a friend" that Linda had met through her charity work who "might" be able to help.

Ted knew exactly what he was doing when Linda's friend turned out to be a known KGB agent working out of the local Soviet Embassy. The KGB officer cheerfully admitted to Ted that it had been his side that had slipped him the documentation. He assured Ted that CIA security officers knew nothing about Linda's past and that they would not find out, regardless of what Ted might decide to do. However, if Ted chose to cooperate with the KGB, then Ted and Linda might live a very happy and well-rewarded life, one in which neither would have to keep secrets hidden from the other, as Linda had been forced to do because of her fear that she would lose Ted if he knew about her past.

Already convinced that socialism was the hope of the future, Ted compared himself to the German who opposed Hitler and the Nazis but not the German homeland, and he agreed to the KGB man's proposal to make a deal in which Ted would be well paid for information he would pass to the KGB.

Ted might have gone on to become another Rick Ames, working his way into promotions that would have made him a valuable mole for the Soviets. But Ted's bad luck held, and for once the CIA's counterespionage system worked like it was supposed to. A year after he started spying, an alert polygraph technician decided Ted was lying during his regularly scheduled polygraph session. At about the same time, one of Ted's colleagues in Peru successfully recruited a spy inside the Sendero Luminoso, and Linda's name turned up in some of his reporting. CIA security officers put Ted under close surveillance and soon arranged a trip back to the United States for what Ted was told would be a training assignment. Once they had Ted and Linda back in the States, the CIA counterintelligence officers planned to arrest Ted and Linda and charge them with spying.

Two nights before Ted and Linda were scheduled to fly to Washington, neither of them apparently aware that they were under suspicion, a truck slammed into their vehicle while they were driving home from an embassy cocktail party. The driver of the stolen truck fled the scene and was never apprehended. Linda was killed instantly. Ted survived for three days of interrogation in a drug-fogged, semiconscious state.

The CIA damage report concluded that Ted had not been spying for the KGB long enough to pass on anything more than tactical intelligence information. The same report also concluded that Linda had been working with the KGB from the very beginning, that Ted had been identified by KGB intelligence officers as a potential recruit, and that Linda had been specifically charged with the recruitment of Ted. It's possible that the KGB somehow learned that Ted was under suspicion and arranged the auto accident to prevent the public exposure of Ted as a Soviet spy, perhaps in order to protect a more important mole already working for the Soviets inside the CIA—no doubt the same person who alerted the KGB that CIA security was on to Ted. It's also possible that it was nothing but a drunk driver causing an accident.

Even when he was disenchanted and discouraged about his career in the CIA, Ted Brennan never considered the possibility of turning traitor until the night Linda suggested that might be the only way they could stay together. If the KGB had not deliberately set out to recruit him, Ted probably would have eventually quit the CIA and taken up a new career. It's possible that he might have turned renegade like

Philip Agee, who also decided that socialism was the hope of the new world and who wrote *Inside the Company: CIA Diary*, an exposé in which he named numerous CIA officers working in Latin America. But it is just as likely that Ted would have faded into the night and spent the rest of his life just as unhappy with a career in business or the international charity industry as he had been with intelligence.

Long before that night when Linda suggested a way for them to be together, KGB intelligence officers had developed an elaborate plan that played on the character weaknesses they had identified in Ted. Linda had probably been on the KGB payroll as an access agent for years and may have been the person who first identified Ted as a potential recruit. No doubt she received considerable training on how to manipulate a man like Ted, and as she led him from casual friendship to a serious romance, a KGB case officer closely monitored her progress.

One might ask why a woman like Linda would agree to play the seducer of a man she neither liked nor respected, even to the point of marrying him and perhaps bearing his children. The answer might be found in the general plight of intelligent but poor women born in any third-world country. The KGB offered a young female university student a way out of poverty, a chance to enjoy an American life-style, and the emotional reward of believing she was on the right side of history. Linda's story is as old as that of Delilah. She may even have eventually convinced herself that she truly loved Ted.

Intelligence case officers consider recruitments like Ted Brennan the epitome of success in the intelligence game, especially since such people already know the way the game is played. As Victor Ostrovsky, the ex-Mossad case officer, explained, "The idea of recruitment is like rolling a rock down a hill . . . you take somebody and get him gradually to do something illegal or immoral. You push him down the hill. We didn't blackmail people. We didn't have to. We manipulated them."

Employing techniques like those used on Ted is considered the best possible way to get a spy in the right place at the right time. Such recruitments allow the intelligence officer to focus on the specific agency or installation where the best information can be found and then to identify someone already in place who might be approached and recruited.

Recruiting someone who is in the right place at the right time is is the preferred method of obtaining spies, but in the real world it is not always possible. Indeed, most government security and counterintelligence agencies are well aware of how spies are recruited and spend a lot of time and effort educating people with security clearances about the methods used by other intelligence agencies, as well as watching for hostile recruitment efforts.

On the other hand, the general public is, for the most part, ignorant of the methods used by case agents to recruit spies. Therefore, the citizen who sets out to recruit spies working for a business competitor, union organization, citizen's political action group, or even government agency that would normally not be the target of a foreign intelligence effort will find much easier targets.

Chapter Six

The Art of Deception

"By Way of Deception Thou Shalt Do War."
—Motto of the Mossad

Recruiting spies is all about deception. The person who spies on his country, employer, friend, or lover engages in a constant deception, pretending to be something he is not—a loyal, honest, trustworthy individual.

The deception doesn't end or even begin with the spy trying to steal secrets. The spy may be as thoroughly deceived by the person who recruited him as the victim of the spy is deceived by the spy.

The spy, the case officer who recruited him, and the case officer's employer may be deceived by the intended victim who is deliberately supplying false information that will lead the enemy into a deadly trap.

The person who wins the game of spying will be the person who is best at deceiving others while at the same time being brutally frank with himself in order to avoid self-deception. Those who practice self-deception will be the biggest losers of all.

ENCOURAGING SELF-DECEPTION:
THE KEY TO RECRUITING SPIES

Everyone wants to think that he is a good person, doing whatever it is he does for the noblest of ideals. Some of the most notorious traitors in history—Benedict Arnold, Simon Girty, Vidkun Quisling, Tokyo Rose, and the Rosenbergs—all thought they were doing noble things. Others, such as the Walker family, Rick Ames, and Richard W. Miller, knew that what they were doing was treason, but they still deceived themselves into believing that they were not doing such a terrible thing and that their sins were justified by their own circumstances and the failure of their supervisors and colleagues to recognize and reward their worth.

The professional intelligence case officer or any private citizen who would recruit a spy must understand the human need for self-justification and be ready to offer believable excuses that the recruit can use for self-deception.

The successful case officer understands the human need for love, friendship, self-respect, and honor, and he will feed those needs as he coaxes a potential recruit into turning traitor. He also understands and plays to all the human weaknesses—greed, anger, envy, sexual desire, and even the fear of God. Like a clever con artist, he will offer to satisfy the human weaknesses while providing the self-justification that allows the recruit to delude himself into believing he is not giving up self-respect and honor.

A good intelligence case officer is someone who would make a good con artist, the kind of person who can call an old lady on the phone and convince her that he is a nice person who wants to be her friend; that she has just won a big prize, but that she must first pay the "gift tax." He will have no remorse or pity for the victim, a person he considers to be a fool, created by God to be cheated.

Most people must be conned into becoming spies. The case officer may have to convince a recruit that he will be spying to bring about world peace when, in fact, the purloined information will be used to win a war. Another recruit may be conned into thinking he is giving secrets to the CIA when they will be going to the KGB.

Those who recruit and manage spies must convince others that they are honest, sincere friends who are only interested in helping the potential recruit solve some problem in his life or win some unexpected reward.

The case officer who intends to recruit and manage spies must practice deception as an art form and a way of life. He must learn to convince others he is something very different from what he really is. He must be able to assume a new identity, spin tales that sound believable, and create an imaginary world that the potential recruit will accept as reality.

Learning to tell believable lies is not something that everyone can do. But anyone who wishes to engage in espionage must learn to tell lies in a way that makes others not only believe them to be true, but to believe them so totally that they will willingly stake their reputations and even their lives on the perceived truth.

Not all people can pull the same con. A good con always works because it fits the personalities of the con artist and the "mark." Anyone directing an intelligence-collection operation must recognize the differences in personalities that can be played against each other. A good case officer must not only be good at deception, he must also be matched to his target and play the role that best fits the target's expectations of whom he can trust.

Good deception, as practiced by the clever intelligence case officer, must combine the skills of a fiction writer with those of an actor. The crafty deceiver must be able to think up a clever lie and then act out the lie as if it were reality. He must be able to adopt and fit into a culture much different from his native culture and play the role as if it were his real life. This is a skill that must be continually practiced. Intelligence agencies dedicate much of the training of the prospective case officer to lying.

How It Works in the Real World

Let's take a look at an example of what we mean when we say that deception is the key to recruiting spies.

Irvin Silverman was a British citizen working as a young bureaucrat in the British Admiralty office that reviewed satellite, signal, and human resource intelligence on the Middle East. Irvin was Jewish, and at one time during his college days he had seriously considered immigration to Israel. He and his wife, Rachel, often talked about this possibility, perhaps after he retired.

Irvin saw no conflict in his sworn loyalty to the crown and his emotional loyalty to Israel, because British foreign policy was generally favorable to Israel. Even so, Irvin was occasionally troubled when he saw intelligence documents with information he thought should be shared with the Israeli Embassy but which carried the restriction that the information could not be shared with any other government.

Several years after starting work for the British government, Irvin and Rachel met Haim Hammer while attending a charity dinner to raise funds to support resettlement projects in Israel. Haim Hammer was a likable Israeli businessman about the same age as Irvin and Rachel, and they soon became good friends. Haim would call the Silvermans every time he visited London. Irvin and Rachel especially enjoyed listening to Haim's descriptions of life in Israel.

One evening Haim complained that while the British government talked a good line, the British Foreign Office often took a less friendly stance at the working level and sometimes failed to pass on critical intelligence to the Israeli government. When Irvin asked Haim how a businessman could know what the Israeli government was getting, Haim answered that besides his business duties, he was a representative of a private group of Jewish citizens spread around the world who helped Jews and Israel in the continued fight for national survival. He assured the Silvermans that he indeed would know whether or not the Israeli government was seeing any specific piece of intelligence, especially intelligence on Arab terrorism and Palestinian plans for action. He then suggested that Irvin might want to put the claim to a challenge by describing some bit of sensitive intelligence so that Haim could determine whether or not the information had been passed to the Israeli government.

The Silvermans, fascinated with the new information on their friend, had lots of questions, and the three of them talked late into the night about Israeli hopes and the continued commitment of many Arab political groups to the total destruction of the Jewish nation. The more they talked, the more Irvin was inclined to accept the challenge to test Haim's claim that much of the intelligence information Irvin saw cross his desk was not being passed on to the Israeli government, apparently because of anti-Jewish sentiment in the British Foreign Office.

Over the next several weeks, Irvin picked out several bits of intelligence that crossed his desk and discussed them with Haim. He was horrified when Haim informed him that the Israeli government had not seen a couple of the reports that did indeed contain critical intelligence information.

Angry about the duplicity of his own government, neither Irvin nor his wife Rachel even considered the fact that what Haim next proposed would be treason—that Irvin regularly pass copies of secret messages to Haim, who would then pass them on to appropriate officers in the Israeli government. Indeed, Irvin and Rachel would have argued that the never named anti-Israeli bureaucrats in the Foreign Office were the ones committing treason by refusing to support what was supposed to be a pro-Israeli foreign policy.

In the months following Irvin's recruitment, Irvin and Rachel would tell each other in their private conversations that Haim's offer to pay for the stolen information had played no role in their decision to help Israel. Even so, the payments quickly built a nest egg that made it possible for Rachel to start the next generation of Silvermans. Once the new baby came, they found themselves increasingly dependent on Haim's cash payments for what they had come to consider necessities.

When Rachel expressed concern about what would happen if Irvin was caught stealing documents, Haim assured them that the Israeli government would help them avoid prosecution. To ease Rachel's fears, he gave them detailed instruction on how they should go to the Israeli Embassy in London at the first indication that anyone was suspicious of them. Haim guaranteed that, if necessary, the Israeli government would smuggle the whole family out of England and into Israel where they would be relocated as heroes of the Jewish nation.

Soon after Irvin entered his fourth year of spying for Israel, he arrived at work to discover two MI5 security officers waiting to interview him about their suspicions that Irvin was making illegal copies of British intelligence documents and passing them on to a third party. Irvin denied the accusation and then insisted that he wanted to seek legal advice before answering any more questions. The security officers agreed that might be a good idea and scheduled a second meeting for later in the day.

As soon as the counterintelligence officers left his office, Irvin left the building, found a public telephone, and called home. Hysterically, Rachel related that four uniformed policemen and two men carrying MI5 identification had arrived at their door carrying search warrants while Irvin was being interviewed in his office. It had been pure luck that the policemen found nothing in their search. The evening before, Irvin had left a load of materials at a drop sight for later pickup by Haim. Otherwise, the policemen would have found the material that Irvin had been hiding in his home for the past several days.

Convinced that his arrest was imminent, Irvin instructed Rachel to take their two-year-old daughter and meet him on the steps of the Israeli Embassy where they would activate the escape plan that Haim had laid out for them so many months before.

Smiling at each other and looking forward to a new life in Israel, the Silvermans were holding hands and Irvin was carrying the baby as they approached the embassy receptionist and Irvin spoke the code phrase that Haim had given him to memorize.

Irvin and Rachel thus began a tour through hell. The memorized phrase not only brought no response from the receptionist, the embassy security officer who finally appeared to talk to them insisted that the embassy had no record of Irvin performing any service for the Israeli government and then ordered the Silvermans to immediately leave the embassy compound.

Back at their home, Irvin worked the telephone while Rachel sat holding the baby, trying not to cry herself as the baby bawled. First, Irvin tried to get through by telephone to someone at the Israeli Embassy who might be more sympathetic to their plight; then he tried calling the different numbers listed on Hammer's business cards as his home and place of business in Israel. In each case the person who answered identified himself as an employee of Mr. Hammer, explained that Mr. Hammer wasn't in the city and promised to pass a message to him as soon as possible. Finally, in desperation, Irvin called the emergency number in Jerusalem that Haim had once written down and handed to Irvin along with instructions that Irvin use the number only in the direst of circumstances. The person who answered on the other end claimed to be a refrigerator repairman who knew nothing about what Irvin was talking about. When Irvin tried the other numbers again, no one answered the phones.

Not knowing what else to do, Irvin called a solicitor and went back to the office for the scheduled second interview with the counterintelligence officers. Irvin realized for the first time just how much trouble he was in when one of the officers showed Irvin and his solicitor a picture of Haim Hammer and asked if Irvin knew the man in the picture. When Irvin hesitated in answering, the examiner again asked the question, this time giving the picture a name, Rashid Yasin, and identifying him as a suspected Syrian intelligence agent.

All the years that Irvin thought he was spying for a private Jewish organization supporting Israel, he was instead passing documents to an intelligence case officer working for a Syrian intelligence agency.

The British government, which doesn't like admitting its failures, opted not to prosecute the Silvermans through the courts or make any public accusations. (It probably would have done so if the officers had found the secret documents that they had hoped to find at the Silvermans' home.) However, Irvin was dismissed from government service. Irvin and Rachel did try to immigrate to Israel, but the British had shared the information on what Irvin had probably passed to the Syrians with Israeli intelligence, and an Israeli Embassy employee told Irvin that the Israeli government might decide to prosecute Irvin for treason if he ever entered Israel.

The False Flag

The man whom the Silverman's knew as Haim Hammer was a Syrian intelligence case officer who had been using a false flag, one of the most important tricks of the intelligence trade used in recruiting spies. Rashid Yasin had been born in Israel but to Arab parents. Recruited as a young man into the Syrian security service, he had spent years perfecting the act that entrapped the Silvermans.

When using a false flag in espionage work, the case officer claims to hold a nationality or be a person whom the target for recruitment will expect to be friendly to the target's own interests. Every intelligence agency in the world uses false flag deception in recruiting spies. A Chinese businessman in Singapore thinks he's working for the Republic of China when he is really spying for Taiwan. A student in Lima thinks he's passing documents to a man from the Cuban Embassy, who is actually a CIA case officer, who was born and raised in Laredo, Texas.

Occasionally, intelligence case officers do identify themselves truthfully to prospective recruits. There are lots of people around the world who would love to work for the Americans and others who would do the same for the Soviets, Cubans, or Israelis. However, even in those situations in which a recruiting officer flies the flag of his true nationality, the initial approach will usually be made by a case officer working under a false identity of some kind. Then, if something goes wrong, the case officer can disappear without a trace.

Although no one collects any statistics on this, the majority of all spies think they are reporting to a different government, political group, or commercial enterprise than the one really reading the information they steal. In most such cases, they would have never agreed to spy for the CIA, KGB, or whoever trapped them into spying. Without the use of the false flag, very little spying would ever get done. The only spies available for recruitment would be political true believers and crass traitors willing to sell out to the highest bidder, no matter who that might be.

The false flag serves two purposes. First, as with the case of Irvin Silverman, it wins the cooperation of a target who might well prefer death to working for the real spy master who will benefit from his traitorous act. Second, it protects the case officer in the event the target refuses to cooperate and reports the attempt to his superiors or is later caught in the act of spying.

Oftentimes, spies who are captured continue to insist that they were working for the organization they thought recruited them long after the false flag has been exposed as a fraud. (The Silvermans still believe that they were spying for Israel and that the claim that Haim was a Syrian spy was a Mossad-inspired ruse to hide their activities in Great Britain from the British. They considered themselves as Jewish citizens whose reputations and economic futures were sacrificed on the battlefield of intelligence collection.)

Because of the security advantages of working a recruitment under the cover of a fake identity, almost all case officers claim a false identity and carry the credentials to support that identity when they approach an individual with the intent of recruiting him as a spy.

Choosing the False Flag

Every attempt to recruit a spy is different, depending on the personality of the spy, the organization or person to be spied on, and the situation under which the spy will operate. A key step in every recruitment is deciding what false flag should be used or, indeed, if any false flag is needed at all.

The false flag must be designed to fit the personality of the person targeted for recruitment and the situation in which the recruitment takes place. The recruiting case officer should represent himself as a person the target will respect, love, or fear.

Sometimes, a false flag character can include all of those things. For example, the recruiting case officer working for a women's rights activist group approaches a devout Catholic working in a government agency that was targeted by the group. The recruiter pretends to be a priest, perhaps a representative of the bishop or a papal agency. The fake priest might claim that the church's interest in the agency is the result of the agency's active support for international birth-control programs using U.S. funds. In fact, the private case officer hopes to gain information that can be used in a publicity campaign criticizing Catholic influence on public policy on birth-control issues.

Pretending to be an authority figure, preferably a feared one, often works well. The recruiting officer might claim to be a special agent of the IRS or the state tax board when approaching the employee of a private company. Another ploy is to claim to be a private investigator or private contractor working for a police or regulatory agency.

On the other hand, if the subject targeted for recruitment is someone who doesn't like authority, then a case officer might choose the cover of being an investigative reporter out to reveal the secrets the agency is trying to hide from the public.

One successful entrepreneur who collected corporate intelligence claimed to be the inventor of an arcane technical improvement in telecommunications equipment. He explained to anyone who listened that the invention had made him so rich that he no longer had to work at a full-time job, but instead traveled around the world looking for interesting investment opportunities.

The recruiter should not only pick a false identity that will appeal to the personality of the target, but one that will justify some interest in the subject of that intelligence-collection effort. The homely secretary of a corporate president might get suspicious if her brand-new boyfriend, who claimed to be an interior decorator, suddenly starts asking about a construction project in Liberia, but not if he had told her soon after they met that he is a civil engineer (as he talks about the bridge he once helped construct in Ecuador).

Remember that the false flag is only one part of the story. A pretty young blonde who meets an embassy official in Paris tells the lonely man she is employed by a German industrialist to look for foreign investment opportunities. As she and the embassy official become lovers, he never suspects that she is really working for the KGB. Yet both the tale of her search for investment opportunities and the lovemaking were part of a carefully thought-out plan designed to recruit the diplomat as a spy.

Deception can even be beneficial when an attempt to recruit a spy fails. If the target goes straight to his security officer to report an attempt at recruiting him to be a spy, he will also carry the tale of the false flag and thus divert attention away from the true identity and intentions of the case officer.

For example, an intelligence officer working for a private business approaches a prospective recruit and claims to be working for the IRS, which would pay a large reward for certain information about the recruit's employer. Instead, the honest employee tells the boss about the attempt. As a result, the target may no longer be such a strong competitor because he's worried too much about an IRS investigation into his financial affairs.

THREE STEPS TO TELLING BELIEVABLE LIES

Everyone lies. It is the most human of all human traits. But some people lie better than others, and the person who recruits spies had better be the best. There are three steps to telling believable lies.

1) Create a well-thought-out story. 2) Set up the necessary props to make the story appear true. 3) Step on the stage and perform the part so well that those listening want to believe the story is true.

Creating a Good Story

Professional case officers call a cover story the *legend*. Like all good stories, a legend must have several elements.

1) *It must contain a lot of truth.* Rashid Yasin/Haim Hammer knew everything there was to know about the operations of various international Jewish groups. He knew how they operated, and he knew that they often recruited Jews in place, including such publicized instances as the Jonathan J. Pollard case in the United States, in which a Jewish organization did indeed recruit an American Jew, who then stole and passed on a collection of intelligence documents.

Keep the lying part of the story to the absolute minimum necessary to achieve the deception. Don't add unnecessary detail that will be difficult to remember and don't elaborate when not required. When someone introduces himself as a doctor at a cocktail party, he doesn't list his qualifications, education, and experience. Indeed, he may be extremely reluctant to talk about his specialty, having too often been approached by strangers who want a little free medical advice.

Nevertheless, the liar must be ready to add additional details if questioned by someone who is curious, or maybe naturally suspicious. When challenged, the trained liar keeps the answers to such challenges as short and to the point as possible. Rather than talking about himself, he asks questions and tries to get others to talk about themselves, their experiences, and their thoughts. The con artist gives the impression of listening sympathetically.

2) *The liar must be familiar with the background supporting the story.* He shouldn't pretend to be a brain surgeon if he doesn't know the difference between a hemostat and hemoglobin. Rashid Yasin knew as much about Israel as any *sabra* (a Jew born in Israel) born and raised near Jerusalem. He also was thoroughly familiar with Jewish religious practices, and he had practiced his deception in dozens of different synagogues in England. When he talked about life in Israel, he sprinkled his conversations with details of streets, stores, markets, theaters, and holy spots that any resident of Israel would recognize. He dropped names of politicians and movie stars and talked about family days celebrating the Feast of the Passover.

3) *The story must give the target some reason to want to listen and believe.* The lie might appeal to the target's prejudices or his curiosity, offer solutions to his fears and personal problems or suggest the possibility of profit.

4) *The lies in the story must be both internally and externally consistent and well thought out.* The teller can't talk at one point about an old car he owns and then later mention the new Ford he drives. In the same way, he should check weather records before talking about getting caught in the rain on the second Saturday last May.

5) *Good lies take advantage of recent events.* When mobs raided the U.S. Embassy in Taipei, Taiwan, the Soviets soon thereafter released several documents through front organizations that claimed to be U.S. secret communications stolen by the mob. Those documents discussed the U.S. government's intention to abandon Chiang Kai-shek, a total prevarication.

When running a deception, a case officer must plan for every possible reaction by the target. He must know exactly what he will do no matter how the target reacts. He identifies the worst possible case scenario, then plans out a response for evey objection, question, or doubt that the target might raise. Once he has the details planned out, he goes over them numerous times before meeting with the target. The better he knows the part he will play, the less likely he will make a mistake.

At the same time, a deceiver must not get so committed to a story that he can not take advantage of new developments or incidents. A good deception plan anticipates almost every chaotic event that might happen. A good lie always starts with a prepared script, but unlike the stage, the liar must be prepared to rewrite the script at each point in the telling.

Setting Up the Props

Every actor needs costumes, background scenery, props, and people who will support his role. It's true that a good actor can sound almost believable just by the way he reads a script, but in espionage, almost is never good enough. The basic props that every case officer needs include such things as documents that support various identities; rented offices with computers, faxes, and phones that will be answered as if they were in a legitimate business office; the right kind of car to go with the story; and the clothes, luggage, briefcases, and personal items that fit the character being played.

The documentation that supports the fake identity can be as complex as a passport, a Social Security card, a driver's license, credit cards, and a complete set of supporting papers such as graduation degrees and professional licenses. In other situations it need not be anything more elaborate than a few business cards and a wallet with a couple of fake ID cards.

There are a number of books on the market detailing the intricacies of false identities, and the would-be case officer should familiarize himself with the literature and then do whatever is necessary to build a collection of identities that fit the personality of the case officer and will stand up to examination. A commercial printer can print a collection of business cards, stationery, envelopes, and invoices with any logo and name the customer requests. Computers with scanners and color printers make it child's play to copy or produce letterheads, company ID cards, club memberships, business licenses, union cards, and just about any other document that will pass cursory inspection.

The person who sets out to recruit a spy in the local union will not need the same kinds of documents that a case officer attempting to cross a border with a fake passport would need. For most private intelligence officers, a good computer and a color printer should suffice for producing all the documentation needed to convince a target that a person is really what he claims to be.

Americans generally accept people for what they say they are, provided they look the part and speak the language. The only time anyone shows identification is when he writes a check, uses a credit card, or is stopped by a traffic cop. Even when someone flashes the credentials of a police officer, a health inspector, or an IRS agent, the target of the investigation seldom takes the time to examine the badge and the ID card closely. Documents that will pass such scrutiny are easily faked and will do the job for most intelligence-recruitment activities.

The background scenery and the support actors should be as well-prepared as the costume and the props. Rashid Yasin/Haim Hammer didn't just carry a fake Israeli passport and a driver's license listing an address in Jerusalem; if someone had called at the address, a woman claiming to be the maid left in charge of the house while Mr. Hammer traveled in England would have opened the door. A call to one of the telephone numbers listed on Hammer's business card was answered by an office secretary anxious to help out a possible customer. There was even a propman ready to pull the curtain closed: the refrigerator repairman on the other end of the emergency number knew as soon as Silverman identified himself that something had gone seriously wrong. He immediately notified Rashid Yasin and his supporting cast that the operation had been blown and that they should all disappear.

Performing the Part

The art of deception is so important to successful espionage that anyone who intends to recruit spies must study and practice deception with the same dedication that an actor demonstrates in his chosen profession. Indeed, I've known several very successful case officers who took part in amateur drama productions so that they could get practice in playing a role with conviction. One of the reasons why Rick Ames may have avoided detection for so long, even passing CIA polygraph exams, is that he studied drama in college and even considered a career as an actor before joining the CIA.

All actors are liars. They are not really in love with the woman; they don't really want to kill the other guy; they are not real cops or robbers. In the same way, all successful liars are good actors. If they claim to be cops, they act and talk like cops would act. The acting is often even more important to a good lie than the other props.

The case officer is always on the stage when he meets with any recruit or potential recruit. As with any actor, the case officer may be playing more than one role as he moves from meeting one recruit to another. He must be able to switch roles with the ease he changes shirts. He can never allow a recruit to catch him out of character, in spite of the fact that he may be running an entire ring of spies, and each spy knows him as a different person.

Chapter Seven

Exercises in Deception and Intelligence Collection

No actor memorizes his lines and then speaks them on the stage for the first time on the night the play opens. Just like the actor rehearses on stage while there is no audience in the theater to boo him, the person who intends to commit serious deception must first practice in situations in which there are no personal risks. However, unlike the actor who rehearses with other actors, the person who wants to recruit spies should practice his deceptive skills in the real world with real people.

The goal of the exercises described below is to learn how to approach a perfect stranger, introduce yourself with a plausible explanation for why you want to meet him, present yourself as someone the stranger would want to know better, and then set the scene so that you meet the stranger in a situation in which you have control. It must all be done while you pretend to be an entirely different character than who you really are.

To practice doing this, approach strangers in such places as hotel lobbies, restaurants, bars, airports, churches, meeting rooms, libraries, grocery stores, roadside rest areas, and any other public places. Initiate a conversation or set a scene where the stranger initiates a conversation and then tell the stranger a story that he believes to be true. The ultimate goal of the exercise is to present yourself with a believable false identity and then to use that identity in a way that gets the subject to reveal something personal, to perform some service for you, or to agree to a second meeting. At the end of the exercise, the stranger should be convinced that he has just met someone who is interesting, honest, and worth getting to know better.

PRACTICING DECEPTION
IN LOW-RISK SITUATIONS

Finding unsuspecting people to practice deception on is an easy task in our society. Most Americans talk to strangers every day, provided they appear to be honest citizens going about their legitimate business or engaging in a popular recreation. We talk to the guy and the gal standing beside us at a bus stop, the person sitting next to us on a plane, the lady waiting on us in a store, people sitting around us at a football game, patrons in the bar where we drink, skiers standing in line at the lift, and in hundreds of other situations. Such conversations may start with some inane comment on the weather but often result in a lot of information being exchanged, especially if one party deliberately leads the conversation in that direction.

Engaging in a harmless deception with a stranger makes it easier from a psychological point of view because you don't have to worry about being found out and then charged with a crime. If a stranger you meet on an airplane accuses you of lying when you tell him you are a writer from some tabloid sold at the checkout stand in grocery stores, it costs you nothing in grief. All you have to do is stop the conversation and think a bit about what made him suspect you were lying.

Don't worry about taking up a stranger's time. Most people live deadly dull lives, and they are usually enthralled when given a chance to experience a vicarious adventure. They will love your tale of how you spent 10 years as a missionary in the Amazon, how you narrowly escaped being convicted of murder, or how much you expect to earn from the sale of your first novel.

Travel Opportunities

When traveling on a plane, train, or bus, board with several different versions of who you are and what you do for a living or a good time. The stories should be worked out in detail, and you should have answers for any questions the target might ask. Indeed, it is a good idea to write down the details of each cover story. Stories might include a claim that you are employed in the movie industry, perhaps as a makeup artist or an assistant to a famous director; that you are a criminal-defense attorney with a long history of getting people off on technicalities; an investor who has made a fortune in a couple of stock deals, and you now spend your time traveling around looking for deserving people to help; a private detective searching for evidence to clear a young woman falsely accused of murder; or a U.S. diplomat on leave after an assignment in some country that has been in the news.

Once you have your stories ready, pick a different one each time you start a new conversation with a new person and tell it as if it were the truth. Start each conversation by asking your seatmate the usual polite queries about his destination, why he is going, etc. If possible, get the other person to talk about himself. That's usually easy to do. Talk about yourself (your legend) only when asked, and then somewhat reluctantly. The more the person talks, the more you will learn about him.

When you do talk about yourself, tailor your story to what you have already learned about the other person. If your seatmate is a pretty, young, serious woman who is a business major at a small university, you might say that you work for a famous movie director. This could lead to questions about whether she has ever taken drama lessons or appeared in any plays. Ask for a name and an address where you might contact her for a possible screen test for a movie you will soon be working on in which the director is looking for new, natural faces.

If your seatmate works for a large international corporation, tell the diplomat-on-leave story. Talk about a number of business opportunities in the country of your assignment, which no American seems interested in.

If the seatmate turns out to be a religious minister, describe your experiences as a defense attorney who successfully defends criminals you know are guilty and often commit terrible crimes afterward. Pretend to be disillusioned and looking for a way to change your life. Throw in a few comments that suggest you've had some major personal problems too—perhaps marital strife or a teenager who has run away from home.

If you are talking to a middle-aged school teacher, pull the detective story, molding it into something that would appeal to the teacher, perhaps that you are trying to clear a high school principal accused of molesting a teenaged boy or to track down a school teacher who travels during the summer as a secret serial killer. If you use this last scenario, try to build the story so that you might use someone like the target as a source. This means you will have to place the investigation somewhere near where your seatmate lives and build it into something that might touch his life. Invent evidence that suggests that the killer might be teaching in a school in his area or that the teenaged boy once went to a nearby school. Ask advice on how you might find out what teachers do during summer vacation. See if you can get the target to agree to do some investigation for you—for good payment, of course.

Other possible identities could include a stock trader if you meet a small businessman; a father searching for a lost child taken by the mother 12 years ago, if you meet some grandmotherly type; a world traveler who's lived abroad for many years, including time spent in a Thai jail for drug trafficking, if you sit next to a college student.

Whatever the cover, the goal should be to get the target interested in what you are doing so that he might agree to help if you asked. You want the target to willingly give you his name, address, and a telephone number where you could contact him for a follow-up. The stranger may ask for the same information from you; give him a false name, address, and phone number. It works even better if you carry several sets of business cards supporting each of the false identities you intend to use.

However the conversation goes, as soon you are alone, sit down and write out all the details of how the deception played out and everything you learned about the target of the deception. Make special note of what went right and what went wrong.

Lying in Church

Go to church in a nearby city where no one knows you. Be friendly and polite to those sitting near you, but sort of shy. Sooner or later, the minister or someone in the congregation will want to talk. Explain how you haven't been in church for many years, but that you had a recent religious experience that made you question your previous agnostic beliefs and sent you looking for answers. Don't volunteer it, but have a detailed story you can relate if asked, perhaps the death of a child, a serious illness, or an experience as a victim of crime or a survivor of some natural disaster. Don't make the experience something miraculous; it should be more psychological in nature. As you talk to various people in the congregation, learn as much as you can about them: where they work, how happy they seem to be with their lives, what different social cliques exist within the congregation, and so on.

How many invitations to social functions, group meetings, or private discussion groups did you get? Whom might you approach if you were an insurance salesman, a man looking for romance, or someone looking for a source to recruit in the local city government? Look for individual quirks and potential character weaknesses that might be exploited should you decide to recruit someone as a spy.

Looking for Business Information

Go to a business office located in a building that overlooks a busy intersection. Tell the secretary that you are an insurance investigator looking for someone who might have seen a fender-bender that occurred several weeks earlier. Mention the possibility of a reward that will be paid to anyone who provides information leading to a witness. Give as few details about the accident as possible in your initial query. It's probable someone will have witnessed some kind of accident during the previous several weeks. If that person gives the details first, you can pretend that what he saw is the accident that you are investigating. Get as much personal information as possible on the people to whom you talk.

If you find someone who is especially interested in the possibility of earning a witness fee, change stories, claiming that you are really investigating the high rate of workman's compensation claims filed by the company and suggest that if the target can provide that kind of information, he might make even more money.

ADVANCED DECEPTION TRAINING

The person who intends to engage in any serious espionage activity, regardless of the target, will want additional training in deception before actually beginning an intelligence operation. These advanced techniques are not innocent fun, as the practice situations above suggested. Even when they do not cross the line of legality, they invite retaliation should the target be able to identify the tormentor. The wise person who uses practice exercises similar to those described below will travel to a distant city where no one knows him, use public phones, and make any long-distance calls by charging the cost to one of the phone credit cards that can be purchased from machines in supermarkets and similar places. He will be training not just in deception but in security as well.

Because these practice deceptions require taking some

legal risks, they should not be engaged in by anyone who does not intend to take up spy recruitment as a profession or a personal necessity.

Some of these advanced training exercises require some supporting false documentation. How much ID is needed and how good it must be depends on the level of deception and the sophistication of the person being deceived. The following exercises assume that you will be carrying whatever documentation might be necessary to back up the deception.

Get Politically Active

Call on the manager of a local political campaign—the more important the office, the better. Using a false identity, claim to be a wealthy volunteer with lots of time on your hands and a sudden interest in politics. Drop hints that there might be quite a bit of money available—if the campaign manager can suggest ways to put the money into the campaign fund without violating federal election campaign laws. Put in several days of work at the headquarters, meeting as many other campaign workers as possible and perhaps even the candidate. The goal is to learn as much information about the candidate's behavior as you can while working with the campaign.

Call a Newsman

Contact a newspaper reporter and claim to be a midlevel government official who has information on a major corruption scheme. (Use the current political situation to come up with a scenario that will make the reporter think he may have the next potential "Deep Throat" on the hook.) Describe the story in detail, providing "evidence" to convince your listener. Suggest a secret meeting in which he will control the security scene. Ask how much the newspaper reporter will pay for the full package of evidence you have.

A Hotel Visit

Check into a hotel with a fake identity, pay cash, and talk to as many people as possible in the lobby, at the desk, in the dining room, everywhere you can. Tell them all the same tall tale—say, for example, that you are visiting the United States on your first vacation in several years after working for a long while as a missionary in a foreign country. During the stay, find out if arrangements can be made with any of the hotel staff for a prostitute to come to your room and how much it will cost. If it's not too expensive, order one, and when she appears, pay her fee (you don't have to actually have sex, unless you want to). Then try to get the prostitute to agree to spy on an important businessman or politician who lives in that city for you.

Using the phone in the hotel room, pick several different businesses, professionals, and government agencies from the yellow pages and call them. With the businesses, pretend to be a customer with a potential big order. With the professionals, try to find out if lawyers will quote fees over the phone, how easy it is to make an emergency appointment with a doctor, or how much free advice you can get by telling a good story. If you are a serious student of deception, you might pretend to be an IRS special agent initiating an investigation of the professional you are calling, or a policeman checking on recent patients who have been treated for a specific kind of injury ("We know the assailant suffered such an injury while attempting to commit rape"). When calling a government agency, report that the business you work for might be in violation of whatever laws and regulations that particular agency enforces; you might also pretend to be a salesman trying to get an appointment with the purchasing agent or a customer asking for a tax identification number in order to file 1099s with the IRS.

Getting into a Stranger's Apartment

Gain entry into a large apartment building by pretending to be a package-delivery service. Carrying a real package, invent a story that will convince a suspicious apartment dweller you are delivering a delivery from an unknown person. Possibilities include flowers sent anonymously or a package containing a small, inexpensive appliance along with a letter on business letterhead explaining that the addressee has been chosen at random for a promotional scheme. (If queried, the deliveryman can explain that he has delivered several such packages around the city.) Whatever the story, you must leave behind someone who believes that he has received a legitimate delivery and will have no reason to call the police or building security officer.

Once inside the building, figure out a way to gain entry into another apartment on a different floor. The cover story must provide you a legitimate reason to be in the building and to request help from someone else inside the building. Cover stories might include a claim that you are a private detective investigating an insurance claim and looking for possible witnesses, a maintenance worker trying to find out who has a certain kind of plumbing or heating problem, or someone who just accidentally dropped a small bottle of wine or soda pop and who would like to clean up the mess before leaving the building.

Gaining Entry to a Private Home

Pick a private home in a middle-class neighborhood and attempt to gain admittance. You might pretend to have car trouble and ask to use the phone. In this scenario, you should have a friend standing by a phone in case the homeowner does the smart thing and leaves you outside while he calls the emergency number you provide. Your accomplice will answer the phone by identifying the number as the Ace Tow Service and then ask the expected questions about the address.

Other introductions that might help you to be admitted into a stranger's house are pretending to be a missionary (remember to carry a Bible and a briefcase full of religious tracts), a federal investigator doing a security clearance on someone who once lived in the neighborhood, a political worker trying to get out the vote, someone collecting for a charity, or a person who once lived in the house as a child and wants to indulge in a bit of nostalgia. The more original the legend, and the better the legend fits the probable prejudices of the homeowner, the better your chance of getting in. Once in, learn as much about the family as you can from your observations and the casual conversations that follow.

All of the above exercises are only suggestions. Each person wishing to practice the art of deception should think up a series of exercises to maximize his strong points. The goal is to get comfortable in the art of lying while in low-risk situations and then move a step at a time into higher-risk situations until you are ready to use your deception capabilities to full advantage to recruit others to steal valuable information for you.

Chapter Eight

It's More
Than Telling Lies

Deception is not enough when it comes to recruiting and managing a spy. The good case officer must be a student of psychology, who understands the human psyche and has the ability to interpret the emotions of another individual and respond to them with apparent sympathy.

BE THE BEST NEW
FRIEND THE TARGET HAS

When victims of con men are interviewed by a police officer they always say something like, "He was such a nice man." Successful con artists and intelligence case officers must learn to act like nice people. They pretend to be sincerely interested in their target, they almost never get angry, and when they do, it's a cold-blooded, well-thought-out action designed to produce a specific behavioral response from the recruit. They ask lots of personal questions (including a few the recruit can answer with a bit of bragging), are sympathetic (never judgmental), and always willing to listen.

A good case officer will use every personal advantage he brings to the contest. People with the physical advantages of youth and good looks will use their sexual attractiveness as an intelligence tool in a manipulation that is as old as the story of Samson and Delilah. An older, educated person will play on the tendency of most people to respect both age and learning. A self-confident, military-style personality will use his charismatic ability to command obedience.

The most effective false flag of all is a beautiful woman or a handsome man who has "fallen madly in love" with the potential recruit. As with the girls of the Easy Come, such a recruiter can often learn the secrets of the recruit without the recruit ever knowing he has become a spy.

In the same way, someone looking like the wise old man may remind the target of an old grandfather. A person who looks like a TV lawyer can offer help and advice, and the motherly woman can win the trust of the young lady who worries about her two-year-old's tantrums or her teenager's fascination with drugs.

PERFECTING THE ART OF CONVERSATION

The intelligence case officer must understand how to get people to talk while he listens. This skill is especially important when using people as inadvertent spies, but it is also a critical skill in the process of recruiting those who will eventually spy knowingly for the case officer. The more the other person talks during any conversation, the more anyone trying to gather information will learn and the less likely it is that the target will learn something that the intelligence collector doesn't want him to know. (A good case officer will never allow the target to learn anything about his true personality, real hopes, fears, or despairs, except when such information fits the false flag he is flying.)

Getting people to talk is much easier than most people realize. Almost everyone would rather talk than listen. Because of that human trait, most social conversations are games in which each side tries to maximize the percentage of time in which he or she does the talking. Few people really listen to what other people are saying. They are instead thinking ahead to what they will say when they next get a chance to take control of the conversation.

As a result, most people are hungry for someone who will listen to them. Both con artists and good intelligence officers know this, and they deliberately feed that hunger. They not only listen, but pay rapt attention and ask questions that encourage the target to keep talking. The best intelligence officer is one who makes the target believe that both of them are important, smart, experienced, and clever, and that the target has something to say that is worth listening to.

Most people so enjoy an intelligent, attentive listener, that they will do everything possible to keep the conversation going. Time and again, I've gotten people to tell me valuable intelligence information by paying them the compliment of listening to every word they say, even when what they are saying is of no interest to me. Even though they may start out with the intention of keeping certain secrets to themselves, as they glory in the experience of having a listener hang on every word, they will start letting slip more and more information in an effort to get the listener to continue to listen to them. People will literally give you their secrets in exchange for continuing to listen to them talk.

I can't count the times I've been in long meetings in which I listened intently as my intelligence source talked about his family, personal experiences, theory of warfare, or political beliefs. Although I learned nothing new, I listened with rapt attention, with my only responses being questions or murmured agreements to demonstrate that I was listening and that I shared his conclusions. Then, when I finally started to apologize for taking so much of the important man's time and suggested it was time for me to go, he would insist that I stay a little longer. When I reluctantly settled back in my chair, he would launch into another monologue in which he did start telling me the secret information I had hoped to get out of him.

One time in Vietnam when I was working as a U.S. civilian official, I interviewed an ARVN (Army of the Republic of Vietnam) lieutenant general on how the war was going in his sector. After spending more than two hours listening to him discuss his theories on the best way to fight the Maoist insurgency—theories that were in total disagreement with those of his U.S. military advisors—I apologized for taking so much of his valuable time and started to stand up to say good-bye. Apparently, I was the first American who had ever taken the time to listen to him without trying to shout him down. He reached a hand out, grabbed my wrist, and pulled me back down to my chair. Then he launched into a long description of a secret cadre assassination program that he and his men were implementing without informing his U.S. military advisors, but which he claimed was decimating the Vietcong cadre in the area.

As he described the program, what most fascinated me was the reaction of his staff who had sat silently through the long meeting, but who were suddenly horrified to hear their general let an American in on their dirty secrets. One captain, the brightest young officer in the group, managed to catch the general's eye to give him one of those glances that attempted to remind the general that he should perhaps be a bit more discreet. The poor captain got back an imperial glare that not only put him in his place, but warned him that he might soon be back in the jungles patrolling for Vietcong ambushes.

What's funny is that when I reported back to my superiors what I had learned, I was told that the general had been feeding me a bunch of lies because what he was telling me was contradicted by the intelligence collected by both army intelligence and CIA case officers. It was only three or four months later that the intelligence experts learned from their well-paid spies what I had learned from the general by paying him nothing more than a few compliments. By then, the ARVN general had been transferred to a dead-end job in Saigon at the instigation of a "ring knocker" (a West Point graduate) advisor who complained to the U.S. command structure that the general was not following U.S. advice on how to fight the war.

THE RULES OF FRIENDLY INTERROGATION

1. Never criticize the other person's religion, country, family, intelligence, education, or personal conduct. If he criticizes himself in any of those areas, be sympathetic to his concerns and confessions, but don't agree with too much enthusiasm.
2. If you disagree with something the other person says and conclude that you must make that point to keep your own credibility, ask questions that give him an opportunity to better explain his beliefs while letting him understand there may be a difference of opinion. Let him know by the way you ask the question that, although you may have doubts about his conclusions, you respect his opinion and want to understand why he believes as he does. Never attempt to use logic to argue him into admitting he was wrong.
3. Answer the other person's questions quickly, simply, and directly. Don't add details and don't anticipate or answer questions he doesn't ask. You want to get back to letting him do the talking as soon as possible.
4. Always follow his question with a question of your own that gets him talking again.
5. If you must interrupt the other person, do so only to ask a question that further expands what he is saying on a subject that interests you.
6. Don't hurry to reach the point of your interview. If possible, let him bring up the subject in which you are most interested. Learn to lead the conversation by suggestion and casual

references. If you do ask direct questions and he seems reluctant to answer, slip into another subject and pretend you really weren't that interested in the matter. Lead him back to the subject after you've softened him up a bit more.

7. Let him fill the silences. A silent break in the conversation makes most people nervous, and they feel compelled to fill it. Use that to your advantage. If the other person doesn't respond immediately to some statement or question, wait him out. If you don't really want to respond to a question he has asked, think about it a moment. He may start talking again to fill the silence.

8. Don't tell lies unless you have already plotted them out as part of a well-planned deception or as part of a carefully crafted cover story.

Anyone who intends to engage in serious intelligence work should practice these rules in every conversation he has in any set of circumstances. I recently bought a used car. While we waited for a minor repair on the car, the salesman and I started talking. By the time we signed the contracts, I knew a surprising amount of inside information about the used-car business and the personal life of the salesman.

The clever intelligence officer does not want to show the world how much he knows or how smart he is; he wants to find out what other people know, how smart they are, and what makes them tick.

TRADE RESOURCES

There are three things that every intelligence agency uses to build the spy's trust in and dependence on the case officer or its agents: money, drugs, and sex. The private intelligence officer must also have access to those three things in sufficient quantities to service the needs of the potential recruit. He must also develop techniques for using each of them in recruiting different personality types.

Cold, Hard Cash

Money comes first because without money, you can't buy sex or drugs. Recruiting spies can be a very expensive proposition. Often, the only way a case officer can get the recruit's attention is by spending money. He will have to buy the proper clothes to fit the personality he is playing, pay for restaurants, entertainment, travel, hotel rooms, rental cars, clothing, technical equipment, and a variety of personal services.

Sooner or later, the case officer will want to offer some payment for the information the recruit is providing. Even when the recruit is spying for ideological reasons, the case officer will want to make payment for services rendered. Getting a recruit to accept money and preferably to sign a receipt stating he has received the money is the final step in any recruitment. Some recruits will agree to spy for the money; some will only accept money as a loan or an incidental reward.

Normally, money will come from those who finance the intelligence-collection activity. Sometimes those who are collecting intelligence will find that they must self-finance the operation. This might include antigovernment groups intent on spying on government agencies as part of revolutionary activity. Because many groups turn to such criminal activities as theft to finance their revolutions, collectors will find that the same techniques they use for recruiting resources can also be used to con unsuspecting people out of cold, hard cash. Such activities are almost always criminal fraud and are beyond the scope of this book.

Drugs
("Candy is dandy, but liquor is quicker.")

The case officer can use a wide variety of drugs in many different ways as a tool for recruitment. If the target has a drug addiction, the case officer might be able to use that knowledge to blackmail him or he might offer to supply the addict with the drug of his choice as a way of making friends or even as a means of rewarding the recruit for services rendered. It may even be possible for the case officer or one of his agents to introduce the potential recruit to drugs and then encourage an addiction which the case officer can later use to his advantage.

Drugs can also sometimes be used as the grease for developing a social relationship or for conducting a subtle interrogation. There is a lot of truth in the old Latin expression *in vino veritas* ("in wine there is truth"). The list of people who have let slip their darkest secrets after consuming a large dose of their favorite mind-alterer starts before the dawn of history and totals in the millions.

Alcohol is always the drug of choice. It is legal in most countries around the world, readily available, and socially acceptable. It relaxes inhibitions, makes people careless, loosens tongues, and impairs judgment. Often the first approach that a case officer makes to a target will be in a situation in which alcohol is being served. Alcohol can be especially useful when dealing with an inadvertent spy—someone who will provide information without realizing he is dealing with the enemy.

Although a case officer will frequently use alcohol and other drugs in dealing with recruits, he must control both his own drinking and the quantity of alcohol consumed by the target during any social occasion. The idea is to get the target under the influence while maintaining your sobriety and without alerting the target to what is happening. There are a number of different tricks of the trade for limiting one's own consumption while encouraging the recruit to indulge more heavily.

Often, especially when dealing with people who have a drinking problem, all you have to do is allow nature to take its course. The drunk will be more interested in filling his own glass than in making sure his new friend is matching him drink for drink. Things get more difficult when dealing with someone who expects that the person on the other side of the table will match him round for round. The tricks of the trade for ensuring that you stay sober while the target gets drunk include the following:

- *Prior to a meeting that will include consumption of alcohol, eat a quantity of fatty food.* For example, eat several pieces of bread heavily spread with butter or a pint of ice cream.
- *Arrange with the bartender to control the drinks, mixing heavy drinks for the target and well-diluted drinks for you.* (This is one argument for doing your heavy drinking in a setting in which you have the control, say a hotel room, a private home, a diplomatic residence, or a bar where the owner or bartenders are on your payroll.)
- *Lift the glass to the lips, but don't actually sip the drink.*
- *As soon as the target's glass is empty, order another round.* Let the waiter take away your still half-full or, better yet, almost full drink.
- *Pretending to be much drunker than you are, "accidentally" spill a full glass.* You can then miss a round while cleaning up the mess.

One of the most difficult tasks associated with the use of alcohol in a social situation is that you must still remember all the details of the meeting so that you can record everything the target says once the meeting is done and you have a chance to be alone. While the drinking goes on, you should use every break in conversation or moment of silence as an opportunity to mentally review the previous conversations and actions as a way of memorizing how you will eventually write the report of the meeting.

Illegal Drugs
Illegal drugs offer even greater opportunities for gaining psychological control of a target than alcohol can, provided you can control the situation. There are several ways in which you can use illegal drugs as an aid to recruitment:

- Build rapport with the target by supplying drugs to feed his addiction.
- Take advantage of his drug-induced state in getting information.
- Make the target's use of illegal drugs a reason for blackmail.
- Get the target hooked on drugs to make him more dependent on you.

The best situation is one in which the target is supplying his own drugs and you simply go along with the situation, taking advantage of developments as they occur.

However, in some situations you may have to play the role of a supplier. You might even use the cover of pretending to be a drug dealer when approaching a known drug addict. The fact that the drugs are illegal makes the case officer and the potential recruit instant co-conspirators in crime. This, in turn, presents future opportunities for blackmail.

Illegal drugs are very much a dual-edged sword. Although they can make the target easier to control, they can also make him more careless as he goes about his spying. A person who uses illegal drugs is also at constant risk of being arrested and charged with drug offense and is notoriously untrustworthy when arrested. Most will immediately sell out their supplier and their friends. Also, an illegal drug user can be fired from any job at any time, especially if the employer randomly tests his employees for drug abuse.

Another major problem with using drugs for recruiting is finding a supply. Case officers working for national spy agencies usually have access to all the illegal drugs. Sometimes they are supplied by the intelligence agency, often from stocks confiscated as part of the government's narcotics-control operations. Sometimes a case officer will use a service agent he has recruited as a source for illegal drugs that can be used in recruiting new agents.

The private intelligence entrepreneur who is working without the protection of legal cover will have to consider the risks in dealing in drugs versus the potential rewards that might result from the use of illegal drugs in a recruitment effort. Frankly, illegal drug use has become such a common occurrence in modern America that intelligence entrepreneurs and private collectors should have little trouble in finding a source for the illegal drugs they may require for successfully recruiting spies. Even so, individuals who have no experience in purchasing illegal drugs or no familiarity with the areas of the city where drugs are openly sold are better advised to look for other ways to subvert a potential spy rather than risk the real possibility of arrest that comes with seeking out a drug dealer.

Although government case officers will drink alcoholic beverages with a target for recruitment, they will not share the illegal drug experience. Indeed, using illegal drugs, even as part of a cover story, is considered reason for serious disciplinary action by the CIA and most other government intelligence agencies.

With the possible exception of an occasional marijuana joint, private intelligence collectors are advised to follow the same practices. This is especially true when it comes to such high-risk activities as sharing needles. When it comes to the use of illegal drugs by a potential recruit, the most important thing is that the recruiter appear sympathetic and nonjudgmental of the use of drugs, and not that he might be willing to share the drug experience.

Because of the major dangers of dealing and supplying drugs, or even being present in places where drugs are used, the case officer must always be operating under a false flag and a well-constructed false identity.

Sex

Sex won't play a role in every recruitment, but it can make a critical difference in how successful many recruitments will be. In almost all situations it should not be the case officer who personally services the sexual desires of the recruit. Indeed, most national intelligence agencies, including the CIA, prohibit case agents from engaging in sexual relations with any recruit. (The exception to that rule may have been the old KGB. There are lots of rumors about men and women who were specially trained in the art of seduction by the KGB.)

Instead of bedding a recruit, the case agent creates and finances a situation in which the recruit finds what he thinks is true love or maybe just more sexual pleasure than the potential recruit knew was possible. If the case agent expects to use sex as part of his recruitment, he will have to also recruit a person who will willingly go to bed with the prospective recruit.

There are several different options for finding potential sex partners for the recruit to enjoy.

Taking Advantage of an Ongoing Affair

Prerecruitment surveillance will often uncover the existence of an illicit sexual arrangement or a budding romance. Almost always, the case officer can take advantage of such a situation, even when it is a legitimate romance. In the case of an illicit affair by a married target, there are usually instant opportunities for blackmail, but the clever case officer may instead choose to become a conspirator in the affair as part of building a relationship with the recruit. The case officer becomes the good friend who helps facilitate the recruit's love life by providing excuses for the target's absence from family duties, perhaps a private place where the recruit can enjoy the lover's attention, or even an opportunity for a double date in which the case officer picks up the cost of entertainment.

There is always the possibility that a case officer can recruit the love interest as his own agent. This is frequently the case in long-term affairs between one married partner and an unmarried colleague. In such situations the single partner is often dissatisfied with the hopeless nature of the relationship and can sometimes be manipulated into spying on the guy she realizes is never going to ask his wife for a divorce.

She may do it as a form of revenge, or she might be convinced that the final result of her perfidy will be a divorce, with her taking the old wife's place in the family mansion.

Obviously, homosexual relations, affairs with underage partners, or kinky sex involving sadism or other perversions can offer considerable opportunities to the case officer who can figure out how to manipulate the situation to his own advantage. Remember that while blackmail is a powerful tool, it works best if the case officer is not the one making the blackmail threat, but rather the one who steps forward to provide an escape route for the target.

Prostitutes

The easiest way to provide sex to a potential recruit is to hire a professional and then set it up to make what happens next appear to be a natural occurrence. A frequent ploy is one in which the case officer makes friends with the target and then invites him out for a night on the town. During the course of the evening, they meet a pair of friendly women, who soon agree to go back to the hotel or safe house where the case officer is supposedly living. How the case officer uses the incident and where it leads will depend on the personality of the potential recruit, whether or not he is married, and, if so, how much he wants to keep the marriage a going concern.

In another ploy, the case officer hires the prostitute, briefs her on what he wants done, and then arranges a chance meeting between the prostitute and the target, with the intention that the target will never know that the shy, innocent girl he met one evening was in fact an experienced lady of the night.

Many higher paid call girls become very adept at acting out roles in situations where the beneficiary of her services is led to believe she is an innocent lover. Nevertheless, if a case officer intends to use a prostitute in this way, he had better give her several trial runs to make sure she can be trusted to do what she is being paid to do. For example, the case officer might set up a test run with a service agent and then have the service agent report back on how well the call girl performed her role.

Once the potential traitor has enjoyed the services of the girl, or for that matter a homosexual prostitute, there are several different ways to take advantage of the situation:

- The prostitute, who has been briefed by the person paying the bill, can probe for information much like the ladies of the Easy Come.
- The prostitute can do things that the target likes so much that he wants to make another date, and another, and then he becomes a regular customer. The potential recruit soon discovers that his new pastime is a very expensive luxury and that he will have to find a new source of income if he is to keep enjoying the pleasure.
- The prostitute plays on the target's sympathy, perhaps spinning a tale of how she is entrapped by pimps, but with only a little help from the target she might escape from her awful life. (This works especially well if the prostitute looks very young and innocent and the target has little experience with professional sex partners.)
- A person claiming to be the prostitute's pimp starts to harass the target, perhaps by claiming that the target hurt the woman during sex and is demanding payment, or by attempting blackmail.
- The prostitute fakes an injury, a sudden illness, or even an accidental death during lovemaking, and the incident threatens to expose the target's activities for the evening.

In each of the cases in which the target finds himself facing a problem, the case officer will be the one who offers a solution.

Anyone who takes up the career of a professional intelligence officer should arrange to have several good prostitutes, both male and female, on tap. How he goes about finding such professionals depends on the country and city where he is operating. Part of the training of any good case officer should be learning the ropes when it comes to finding a willing prostitute. The case officer will, of course, always make any contacts with professional sex partners under a cover identity.

Using a Service Agent

Every good case officer will have several agents he has recruited to work for him, not for the intelligence they can steal but rather the services they can provide. This can include providing sexual services to those targeted for recruitment—provided the case officer can find some attractive young person who is willing to make the easy sacrifice for his country, the team, the political leader, or whatever other false flag the case officer is flying when he recruits the young person.

It's relatively easy to find young men who will seduce a woman for the good of their country or just a good paycheck for services rendered (even if she may not be much of a catch), but sometimes a case officer can find females just as anxious to do their part for their country or their political ideals.

The case agent uses the same techniques to recruit a volunteer sex partner as he would for recruiting a primary agent. For example, a CIA case agent might recruit a young female college student in a northern European country by promising to help her get a work visa in the United States if she will first seduce the son of the deputy prime minister. In another situation, the case officer might convince a pretty tree hugger to bed an executive working with a logging company to get evidence that can be used in a lawsuit to halt clear-cutting. (The information will really be used by a competitor logger to undercut a bid for a Forest Service log sale.)

In the following example of using a service agent as a sexual agent, Doug Kranz worked as an information specialist for a Washington lobbyist doing business with the transportation industry. Kranz was looking for a good spy inside the Interstate Commerce Commission and had identified Martha O'Conner, a secretary working in the office of a deputy commissioner, as a potential recruit. Kranz's surveillance had discovered that Martha occasionally went barhopping with a few female friends in the singles joints of Georgetown, but that the homely and overweight woman always went home alone, though her prettier friends often got lucky.

Fat, 40, and bald, Kranz knew he had little chance at building any kind of personal relationship with Ms. O'Conner; however, he had another recruit sitting in the wings, waiting for just this kind of a problem. Dick Ford, a graduate student at American University, knew Kranz as David Fraser, the executive director of the Air Quality Education Council, an environmental protection political action group supposedly based in Denver, Colorado. Kranz/Fraser explained to Dick Ford that his organization wanted better access to the office where Martha O'Conner worked and would pay a substantial sum of money for such access. Dick, whose serious financial straits were about to force him to drop out of grad school, agreed to take on the job that the man he knew as David Fraser was offering.

The next time Martha O'Conner went along with her friends on a tour of the Georgetown bars, it was Martha who got lucky. At Kranz's instruction, David bedded Martha several times over the next several weeks before taking the next step. When Martha was totally committed to him and the pleasure he was giving her, Dick told Martha he was going to have to drop out of school and return to his home state because of his financial problems. He then mentioned one possibility that might keep him in town and in Martha's bed. He had a friend working with an environmentalist group that would pay good money for a bit of inside information Martha might provide.

Martha was soon hooked, and for the next two years she passed increasingly sensitive executive branch documents on to Dick, who passed them to the man he knew as David Fraser. Both Martha and Dick believed that the information that Martha was stealing was helping an environmental group fight attacks on automobile pollution controls, when, in fact, Doug Kranz's boss was using the information in his lobbying efforts for less restrictive legislation and in recruiting new businesses by scaring them with insider information on what new regulations were coming down the pike.

The Innocent Amateur

If some situations, the case officer might identify a potential love partner he introduces to the target, or arranges for the target to meet, and then let nature take its course. Once love develops, the case officer deliberately creates a situation that places the future of the lovers in jeopardy. Eventually he offers a solution, but the potential recruit must steal a few harmless documents first.

In the early 1960s, Czech intelligence officers succeeded in recruiting a U.S. diplomat stationed in Prague by using such a technique. The primary case officer, Jaroslav Parma, had identified the diplomat, Edwin Trickett, as a man with a roving eye for the ladies. Trickett also had a wife with whom he often argued. Jaroslav found a pretty, young Czech woman, Patricie, who had applied for an exit visa to visit a brother living in the United States. The Czech government had denied the visa, the usual practice in those Cold War days.

Jaroslav arranged a situation in which Patricie "accidentally" overheard two strangers talking in a library about how one way to get a Czech exit visa was to have someone from the U.S. Embassy contact the Czech government. One of the strangers mentioned that Edwin Trickett, the administrative officer at the embassy, had done several such favors for pretty young women. The second stranger said he understood that only worked if the young women were willing to "do anything" to get a visa.

Patricie, who so badly wanted to escape life in Czechoslovakia that she would indeed do anything, acted on the gossip she had overheard. She called the U.S. Embassy and asked for an appointment with Edwin Trickett. Trickett, who in truth had never traded intervention on a visa matter for sex, had no way of helping her out but was still intrigued by the pretty Czech woman who seemed so anxious to do anything to get a visa. Rather than simply telling her she had bad information, he promised he would try to find a way to help her get the exit visa and suggested that they meet in a few days so he could report what he had found out.

Although he was initially suspicious about Patricie's motives, her innocent demeanor and adamant criticism of the Czech socialist government soon convinced him that she really was what she claimed to be. They met several more times outside the embassy and eventually became lovers. After that, Trickett did seriously start looking for ways in which he might help the young woman get out of the country. As his marriage was floundering he even began considering the possibility that he might divorce his wife and marry Patricie.

Eight weeks later, Edwin was heading for a little afternoon delight with Patricie when he saw several policemen coming out of Patricie's apartment building, dragging Patricie with them. Terrified at what he had witnessed and certain that his illicit romance was about to be exposed, Edwin spent a miserable two days waiting for the second shoe to fall. On the third day he received a call at his embassy office from someone calling himself Jiri, who claimed to be Patricie's uncle and who demanded a meeting with him.

When they met, the uncle told Edwin that Patricie had been charged with spying for the Americans and that Edwin was going to be named as the intelligence officer who was her control officer. Jiri, who claimed to be an upper-level bureaucrat in the Ministry of Industry, explained he had pulled a few strings and arranged to meet with his niece in her cell. She had vehemently denied she was a spy but had admitted her affair with the U.S. diplomat. Jiri had pulled more strings and was hopeful that he could get the charges against his niece dropped, provided that Edwin was willing to meet with a Czech security officer and convince him that Edwin was not a

CIA officer but a legitimate diplomat. If Edwin failed to convince the security officer of that, then Patricie would be tried as a spy. The Czech government would also declare Edwin persona non grata and expel him from the country. That, in turn, would expose Edwin's affair to his employer, co-workers, and family.

Edwin agreed to such a meeting. The security officer with whom he met was, of course, Jaroslav Parma. Parma grilled Edwin for several hours about his work as an administrative officer in the U.S. Embassy. Edwin's embassy job was, in fact, a dull administrative job that had nothing to do with either policy or the collection of intelligence.

As Parma listened to the diplomat talk about his daily drudgery, Parma became friendlier and friendlier, assuring Edwin that he believed what Edwin was saying. Over the next two weeks, Parma arranged for three more meetings so that he could gather more details, explaining that while he was convinced that Patricie was innocent, he still had to convince his superiors of that. Parma also warned Edwin that he should not tell anyone in the embassy about his problems, because that would only make it more difficult to arrange Patricie's eventual freedom—advice that Edwin was only too anxious to follow. Finally, in the third week, Parma arranged to allow Edwin to visit Patricie in the jail.

Left alone with Patricie in her cell, Edwin listened to the terrified woman as she described her interrogation by the Czech security police. Yet, even though near hysteria, Patricie pleaded in whispers with Edwin that he not do anything for the Czech government. She insisted that Edwin forget he ever knew her and that he get out of the country as soon as possible. Patricie's obviously sincere concern for Edwin and her willingness to sacrifice her own life only helped to convince Edwin that he must do everything possible to help the woman he loved.

Edwin left the jail absolutely certain that Patricie was an innocent victim, which in fact was true. In his next meeting with Parma, the Czech security officer assured Edwin that things were moving in the right direction. The only problem was that he needed something extra to convince his superiors that Edwin was sincerely trying to help the young Czech woman. He suggested that it would be very helpful if Edwin could provide a few embassy documents for Czech intelligence. Parma assured Edwin that the documents didn't have to be classified, but rather could be something as common as personnel and administrative manuals. Parma promised that with just a bit of cooperation, Edwin could solve both Patricie's legal problems and also avoid the exposure of his little love secret.

The next time he met with Parma, Edwin took with him a complete set of U.S. State Department's administrative manuals. While they were marked *Official Use Only*, they were typical bureaucratic rules and regulations of personnel conduct and administrative procedures for letting contracts out for bid, signing rental agreements, ordering supplies, running the embassy commissary, and hiring local employees.

Two days later, Jaroslav Parma told Edwin that Patricie had been released into her uncle's custody. Parma warned Edwin that the case was still not closed and suggested that it might be necessary for Edwin to again demonstrate his willingness to cooperate with the Czech government. Jaroslav then promised that if Edwin would continue to cooperate until his tour in Prague was up, the Czech government would grant Patricie an exit visit, which would allow her to leave the country for the United States.

Edwin's wife had recently returned to the United States for a vacation with her aging parents, so Edwin was able to spend Patricie's first night out of jail with her at her uncle's house. Once they were alone, Patricie again pleaded with Edwin to do nothing to help the Czech government and to forget about her, advice that Edwin refused to accept.

Happy to have Patricie free, and optimistic that he would succeed in eventually getting her out of Czechoslovakia,

Edwin was an easy mark for the next step in his recruitment. For the next several months, each time Edwin passed Parma a new set of documents, the security classification stamped on the documents crept a little higher. While Edwin did not normally have any reason to see classified material as part of his job description, his responsibilities as the embassy administrative officer gave him easy access to all sections of the embassy, including the classified document storage areas.

Who knows how long it would have gone on if Edwin had been a bit more cautious. But the embassy security officer noted that Edwin was spending a lot of time in the classified-document storage vault and got suspicious. He did a bit of police work, and Edwin got caught. Edwin was charged, convicted of treason, and sentenced to a long prison term in a federal penitentiary in the United States. No one on the U.S. side knows what happened to poor Patricie.

Chapter Nine

The Case Officer at Work

L et's take a look at a successful recruitment from
start to finish, using an example that dates back to
the Cold War when the new Communist govern-
ment in Cuba was expanding its influence in Latin America.

The CIA policy staff, with the approval of the National
Security Council, determined in the mid-1960s that more infor-
mation was needed on Cuba's subversive activities in
Venezuela. The policy staff asked that the CIA station in
Caracas identify and recruit someone working inside the Cuban
Embassy in Caracas who might provide such information.

The CIA station chief in Caracas assigned a case officer,
Harold Doyle, the responsibility for doing so. Doyle was already
running a surveillance operation on the Cuban Embassy out of
an apartment building across the street from the embassy. The
surveillance had identified several Venezuelan nationals who
worked in the embassy, including Tomasina Lopez, who
worked as a cook in the embassy cafeteria.

Helena Chavez, a Venezuelan national, was working for
Doyle as an access agent. Helena was a middle-class college
dropout who had long been fascinated with American movies,
fashions, and men. She had been working as an employee of
the CIA for four years. Although she considered it a good job

with good pay, the work also gave her access to the U.S. male diplomats working in the embassy, one of whom she hoped might eventually fall in love with her and propose. Helena had once gone to the United States for four months of CIA training and was regularly "fluttered" (polygraphed) to ensure her loyalty to her employer.

Helena approached Tomasina Lopez while the latter was attending mass and made friends with her. Helena learned that Tomasina never left the embassy kitchen while she was working and that she knew almost nothing about the Cuban nationals who worked in the embassy. Tomasina was not a good prospect for recruitment as either a primary agent or an access agent.

However, Helena also learned that Tomasina had an adult son, Jorge, who was desperately looking for work. Tomasina complained in her conversations with Helena that it was too bad that Jorge wasn't a better driver because the Cuban Embassy was looking for a new chauffeur.

A surveillance of Jorge found him to be in desperate straits indeed. He owed money, his wife was about to produce their second child, and he had been blacklisted by a foreman of a U.S. oil company where he once worked after he had been caught distributing pro-Castro propaganda sheets to fellow workers. Helena arranged to meet Tomasina while she and her son were walking together on the street and was thus introduced to Jorge.

A couple of days later, Helena "accidentally" bumped into Jorge in a crowded department store. Pretending to find Jorge an attractive male who interested her, Helena accepted Jorge's quick invitation to share a *cafecito*. After sounding him out during several subsequent meetings over coffee and verifying that he was ready to do about anything to earn money, she introduced Jorge to Harold Doyle, again in what appeared to be a chance encounter. Harold, using the name Brent Stoker, pretended to be a Canadian journalist who was writing for a leftist news magazine and who was looking for victims of

U.S. imperialism to write about. Jorge was only too happy to spill his tale of woe about his mistreatment at the hands of an American-owned company.

In appreciation of Jorge's contribution to the story he claimed to be writing, Harold paid for Jorge to take a week-long driver's education course, as the only student of a special tutor. As soon as Jorge finished the course, Tomasina asked her supervisor in the Cuban Embassy to help get Jorge the job as an embassy driver.

Once Jorge was working in the Cuban Embassy, Harold—or Brent Stoker as Jorge still knew him—suggested that Jorge could help him with a new story, one trying to put a human face on the Cuban diplomat working in Venezuela. All Jorge would have to do was report on what diplomats talked about while riding around in embassy cars. A promise to pay off Jorge's debts if the information proved useful convinced Jorge that he could help the friendly journalist gather that kind of information without compromising his loyalty to his new employer. Joking that his Cuban employers might get suspicious if they saw Jorge meeting with a gringo, even a Canadian gringo, Harold suggested that Jorge pass on whatever information he overheard to Helena.

One of Harold's support agents rented an apartment in a lower-class housing area, where Helena took up residence. Jorge began visiting Helena once or twice a week for what would appear to anyone following him to be for romantic purposes. Helena, on her own initiative, began bedding Jorge during his visits as well as debriefing him while they showered together on what he had learned while working in the Cuban Embassy. After he left, Helena would write up the information and pass it on to the U.S. Embassy case officer.

Because he was earning two incomes and getting lots of sex on the side while his wife recovered from the birth of their second child, Jorge didn't spent a whole lot of time worrying about the identity of the mysterious Canadian. While he learned nothing of immediate intelligence value on the job, he was learning a lot about the Cuban diplomats, mostly by listening to the gossip of embassy wives he often drove on shopping excursions and trips to charity events.

One of those wives, Dora Martinez, was married to a first secretary in the Cuban Embassy, Silvestre Martinez. On several occasions Jorge drove Silvestre to parks and other public places where Silvestre would meet with Venezuelan students and other Venezuelans who appeared to be ordinary workmen. This activity suggested that Silvestre was working with student and labor groups. He would have exactly the kind of information that Harold Doyle was hoping to collect.

Jorge also reported through Helena that Silvestre Martinez was not getting along with his immediate supervisor and that the embassy gossip was that Dora Martinez was sleeping with the supervisor.

All this suggested that Silvestre Martinez might be recruited as a spy, if he was handled the right way. Harold Doyle, the station chief, and other CIA colleagues began to plan out how the approach would be made and agreed that Doyle would make the approach using the cover of a Canadian journalist.

Before they could initiate the plan, Jorge overheard two senior Cuban Embassy officials, one of whom was Silvestre's supervisor, discussing how they planned to transfer Silvestre Martinez back to Havana. One of the careless diplomats also let it slip that Silvestre's wife, who held an embassy position as a secretary, would remain in place in Caracas, at least for several months. Even Jorge could figure out that Silvestre was getting a career shaft so that the supervisor could have easy access to the wife.

Harold Doyle discussed the situation with the station chief, and after an exchange of telegrams with CIA headquarters in Langley, Virginia, they decided they did not have enough time before Martinez's transfer back to Cuba to carry out the usual recruitment procedures, which can often take weeks or even months. Instead, Harold would try a cold pitch.

(Although seldom used as a recruitment technique and almost never successful, a cold pitch is a direct approach with no prior contact. Someone walks up to the potential recruit while he is in a public place and makes an offer that, it is hoped, the target will find too good to turn down.) A cold pitch is used only as a last resort, but this did appear to be the kind of situation in which there was no other choice, especially since none of the other diplomats in the Cuban Embassy offered likely prospects for recruitment.

Harold approached Silvestre Martinez while they were both attending a National Day Party at the Mexican Embassy in Caracas. Catching Martinez alone for a moment in a roomful of people, Harold started the usual chatter that makes up so much of the inane conversation at diplomatic entertainment functions. Halfway through the second sentence, when he was sure no one was listening, he dropped his voice to a whisper, moved his face closer to Martinez, and in a half-dozen short sentences made an offer. He let Martinez know how much they knew about him and about his wife's affair with his boss—news that apparently Martinez suspected but didn't know for sure. Doyle then suggested that the best way Martinez could take revenge would be to accept an offer of a lump-sum payment of $20,000 and a regular income deposited in a Swiss bank account for passing on information to the Americans during the time Martinez still remained in Venezuela.

After Martinez returned to Havana he would become a U.S. mole inside the Cuban Ministry of Foreign Affairs. While Martinez spied for the Americans, his Swiss bank account would grow. Harold promised that after 10 years the CIA would smuggle Silvestre out of Cuba so he could enjoy his wealth in Miami.

Martinez must have already figured out what was happening to him and his career and had been considering possible alternatives. He immediately rejected the suggestion that he return to Havana as a mole and instead proposed that he defect, provided the Americans made a lump sum payment of $30,000 and set him up with a new identity in any American city he might choose. In return, Martinez would tell everything he knew about Cuban foreign policy and propaganda efforts in Latin America. Martinez also insisted that there must be no public announcement of his defection. He wanted to simply disappear.

Doyle was not surprised at the counteroffer. It was one of the possibilities they had planned for, even down to how much they might offer as payment (Martinez could have gotten $50,000, if he had insisted). Doyle agreed and suggested that the defection take place that very evening. When Martinez nodded his head in agreement, Doyle described a taxi that Martinez would find parked on a street near the embassy and suggested that Martinez might want to go find it.

The entire conversation had taken less than five minutes. The two men walked off in different directions, and two minutes later, after a few brief words with another American colleague, Harold Doyle was listening to a vacuous explanation of Venezuelan politics offered by a half-drunk Peruvian diplomat.

Martinez didn't talk to his wife before he slipped out to find the taxi waiting to take him into exile. The taxi took Silvestre Martinez to a safe house in the suburbs where he spent the next three months with CIA debriefers. During that time, the Cuban Embassy frantically searched for the missing diplomat. On several occasions, its spokesmen made public demands that the Americans tell them what had happened to Martinez, but they had no proof that the U.S. Embassy had been involved in Martinez's sudden disappearance.

Jorge heard dozens of different rumors discussed in the backseat of the embassy car he drove, including one wife suggesting to a friend that Silvestre's supervisor had arranged to have Silvestre kidnapped and killed because Silvestre had found out about the supervisor's love affair with his wife and threatened to go public with a complaint.

CIA interrogators prepared several hundred pages of

raw data based on the lengthy debriefing of Silvestre Martinez. The station reports officer then reduced the data to several dozen intelligence reports and forwarded them to CIA headquarters.

With the debriefing completed, the station sneaked Silvestre Martinez out of Venezuela on board one of the U.S. Air Force Boeing 707s in the executive fleet. The aircraft had flown a group of U.S. Congressmen to Caracas for an inspection on the progress of U.S. economic assistance programs.

Today Silvestre lives in Miami. He has a new name, a new wife, a new career, and he avoids anything having to do with politics. Everyone who knows him as his new identity, including his new wife, thinks he was once a utility worker who fled Cuba on a raft.

A dozen different CIA analysts working under the direction of the deputy director for intelligence (DDI) reviewed the intelligence reports on the debriefing of Silvestre Martinez. The information was condensed into a four-page intelligence dissemination report, which was then edited and rewritten a half-dozen times.

The staffers in the CIA responsible for the final dissemination of the report on this operation were not happy with the results. First, they criticized the station and Doyle for not convincing Martinez to remain in place. They also criticized Doyle for allowing Martinez to defect without a public announcement. But what most bothered the Washington wizards was that the information provided by Martinez didn't support the U.S. foreign policymakers' own beliefs about Cuban diplomatic activities in Latin America.

Although Martinez had confirmed that the Cuban government was committed to spreading revolution in Latin America, he described the Cuban diplomatic effort as inept, incompetent, and disorganized. He portrayed the Cuban diplomatic corps as a collection of competing careerists who were frightened of their own security investigators and incapable of taking advantage of new opportunities that occasionally developed in host countries.

Because most of the CIA intelligence reporting in that area described the Cuban revolution as a major threat to the development of democracy in Latin America—a threat that required a massive infusion of both economic development assistance and covert political action—the agency's bureaucrats decided that Silvestre Martinez must have been a disinformation plant. They therefore limited the dissemination of the report to a few top-level policymakers within the intelligence community, with a caveat as a cover sheet, warning that the information might not be reliable. In so doing, they demonstrated the basic principle that *good intelligence has no value if the recipient is not willing to act on that which proves the recipient's previous beliefs were wrong.*

Chapter Ten

When a Private Citizen Recruits

Now that we have seen how government espionage agencies work, let's take a look at how a
person with no connection to any government or
political group can spy successfully. This example involves
the simplest kind of spying: a situation in which one individual wants to know what another individual is keeping secret.

Janet Thompson suspected that her husband, Bill, was
having an affair with his secretary, Mandy Shumway, and that
he might be planning on leaving Janet and her two teenaged
children. Bill was the owner/manager of a real estate investment firm worth several million dollars. Janet would have
happily given Bill a divorce, provided that she got half the
value of his business (something guaranteed by the
community-property laws of the state where they lived). She
feared, however, that Bill might be moving funds out of the
firm into secret bank accounts and that she would wake up
one day to find Bill long gone, leaving her nothing but a company stripped of cash and facing bankruptcy. On the other
hand, if Bill was engaged in nothing but a short-time fling,
Janet was willing to let the flame burn out—provided the
company profits kept rolling in.

Because Bill was well known in the community, Janet
didn't want to discuss the issue with a local lawyer or private

detective, for fear that Bill might learn about her suspicions and take preemptive action. Janet instead discussed her problem with her brother, Ted Monet, a career military officer who was assigned as an assistant air force attaché in the U.S. Embassy in Singapore and who was visiting the United States on home leave.

Ted, with three more weeks of leave on his hands and already bored with staring at the lake in front of his vacation cabin, decided to make it a busman's holiday by practicing a few of the skills he had learned as a military intelligence officer. He called two old military buddies and invited them and their wives down to share the lakeside house where he was staying, explaining the entertainment he was setting up for the occasion as an extra enticement. Both the couples arrived two days later, anxious to get on with the spy game Ted had promised as a diversion.

Ted assigned one of the two couples, Sylvia and Terry Mineta, to a full-time surveillance of Mandy. The other couple, Dawn and Craig Wallop, began a surveillance of the investment firm with the intention of identifying possible sources working for the husband who might report on what was happening inside the company.

Sylvia and Terry quickly confirmed that Bill and Mandy were engaged in a hot and heavy romance, often taking long lunch hours together as well as spending lots of time in the office "working late" after the other employees went home. They continued the surveillance while looking for a possibility of a *chance* meeting with Mandy and Bill when they were together.

Craig and Dawn, using information provided by Janet, identified three people who worked at the firm who might know something about how Bill was managing the cash flow. One of the employees, Mark Weiss, attended the local Methodist church with his family every Sunday morning. The Wallops also learned that the Weiss couple were avid duplicate bridge players.

The Wallops went to the same church the next Sunday, telling everyone they met that they were planning to move into the area. They met the Weiss family and quickly "discovered" a mutual interest in duplicate bridge. Mrs. Weiss not only suggested that the Wallops come to their next bridge game, but also invited the new friends home for a Sunday brunch.

By the time the four people got to the dessert, Craig had let it slip that he was looking for some investment property and that the planned move to the city depended on what properties might be available. Mark readily volunteered the fact that he was associated with a real estate investment firm and then let it slip that he wasn't very happy in his job. Answering a few friendly questions, he explained some of the reasons why, including vague references to some strange investment moves by the company president.

Craig, dropping hints that he might have a lucrative employment opportunity for Mark if things worked out, got Mark to talk in more detail and learned that what bothered Mark most about his job was that Bill had recently made a number of business decisions on mortgages and property sales that didn't make a lot of sense in the current market.

Ted spent his time at the local county courthouse, collecting all the available information on the properties that were owned or managed by Bill's company. Ted discovered that new loans had recently been taken out on several pieces of property for the maximum amount possible, while the bank loans on three other pieces of property had shortly thereafter been paid off.

Next, Ted spent a few hours with a desktop computer, a scanner, a color printer, and several packages of plastic identification card cover material. Armed with a complete set of fake documents, he called at the escrow company that usually handled the escrow accounts of Bill's company. Announcing himself as a special agent for the IRS and flashing documents to prove it, Ted was ushered into the manager's office. The manager quickly agreed to cooperate with the investigation Ted claimed he was conducting on Bill's company.

With the manager's cooperation, Ted learned that an escrow account had been opened on one of the pieces of property on which the outstanding loan had recently been paid in full. The closing date was set for September 15, just two weeks away. Ted pulled his same act with the two other escrow companies in the area. He found an escrow account had been opened on another piece of property in one of the companies with the same closure date. The manager at the third escrow company refused to release any information, insisting that Ted first get either a search warrant or a court subpoena.

Promising he would immediately do so, Ted suggested he would rather not go to the trouble if there was nothing to subpoena. The manager then confirmed that if the IRS agent presented a subpoena, he would get records of interest. Ted thanked the manager and left, now certain that Bill was going to sell three pieces of mortgage-free property on the same day for a combined total of something in the neighborhood of four million dollars.

Sylvia and Terry followed Bill and Mandy one evening to a small French restaurant located in a nearby city. Sylvia and Terry also ate in the restaurant, sitting at a table near Bill and Mandy, but paying attention only to each other. The Minetas left the restaurant a few minutes before Bill and Mandy and then spent some time necking in their car, breaking up the session with just enough time to deliberately crash their car into Bill's as he and Mandy drove out of the parking lot.

Profusely apologizing and accepting full responsibility for the accident, Terry offered to pay all the repair costs, provided Bill didn't call the police or involve the insurance companies. Playing the frightened man afraid he's about to be found out, Terry confessed that he and Sylvia were not married to each other. While Terry arranged to pay for the repairs to Bill's car (giving a fake address to which Bill was supposed to send the repair bill), Sylvia started talking to Mandy, tricking her into admitting that she was in the same situation as Sylvia—dating a married man, with all the troubles that go with the territory. Sylvia suggested to Mandy that the two of them ought to get together once in a while to keep each other company. Like most women dating married men, Mandy spent a lot of lonely evenings while Bill was home with his family. She jumped at the chance for a new friend who understood and sympathized with her situation.

Sylvia invited Mandy to dinner the next evening that Bill stayed home with his family. Sylvia monopolized the early part of the conversation by telling a tall tale about her hopeless situation; she knew her lover was never going to divorce his wife. When Sylvia suggested that Mandy's situation was probably just as hopeless, Mandy bragged that she was much luckier, adding that she and her lover were about to elope. Although not giving all the details, Mandy explained that Bill and she would soon leave for New Zealand, where they were going to start life over as a married couple under a new identity. Mandy added a long rationalization for why Bill was justified in abandoning a bitchy wife and two spoiled teenagers who had no respect for their father.

Putting everything together, Ted knew that Bill was indeed going to elope with Mandy. He planned to take the payments for the three pieces of mortgage-free property and transfer the funds to foreign bank accounts and then jump the first plane to New Zealand, where he expected to live out the rest of his life with Mandy. Janet would not only be left with nothing but a bankrupt company, she would also probably be stuck with the responsibility of paying off the capital gains taxes on the properties Bill sold.

When Ted presented Janet the evidence he and his friends had discovered, she hired a lawyer who took immediate action. Two days before Bill expected to finalize it all and head for New Zealand, a process server handed him a collection of subpoenas that would not only take him into court for divorce proceedings but prohibited any monetary withdrawals from the escrow accounts until after the property settlement.

The first time they met in a courtroom, Janet twisted the knife a bit by telling Bill that it was his girlfriend who had blown the escape plan by talking too much to a new friend.

In the final settlement, Janet got most of the money from the escrow accounts, Bill got stuck with the heavily mortgaged properties in a falling real estate market, and Mandy moved to another state without giving Bill her new address.

IS SPYING WORTH THE TIME, MONEY, EFFORT, AND RISK?

That's the question everyone considering spying on someone else must ask. For Janet, the answer was obviously yes. By spying on her husband, his business, and his girlfriend, Janet was able to take timely action that saved her and her two children from severe economic and emotional distress. Furthermore, she obtained the information at a minimum cost because of her brother's expertise and his willingness to not only work for free himself, but to recruit four others to work with him. Her brother did take what some would describe as an unacceptable risk when he pretended to be an IRS special agent, but even that risk was minimal in that Ted made only three calls on three different people on the same day while using the fake ID. He never made any further contact with the people to whom he showed the computer-generated fake credentials.

Spying Alone Won't Guarantee Victory

Many historians and critics of the U.S. intelligence effort through the Cold War agree that the KGB won the spy war in the field of covert information collected by using recruited spies. Over the years, the KGB and its allies achieved repeated success in recruiting spies like Whittaker Chambers, the Rosenbergs, Kim Philby, John Walker, Richard W. Miller, Aldrich Ames, and, of course, U.S. Marine security guard Sgt.

Clayton J. Lonetree. (These and others were all found out. We must assume there were many more spies for the Soviet government who were never discovered.)

On the other hand, the CIA was notably unsuccessful in their attempts to recruit spies inside either the Soviet Union or any of the Soviet bloc countries. (Those good spies we did get were mostly walk-ins, and most of those were eventually exposed by the spies the KGB recruited from our side.)

The reasons the CIA failed so miserably in recruiting good sources inside the Soviet Union and Soviet bloc countries are many. One obvious impediment was the difficulty of gaining access to potential spies in a tightly controlled totalitarian system that puts severe limitations on personal freedoms. The Soviet government watched its citizens, especially those with access to government secrets, in ways that can never be employed in a free society. For the Soviet citizen, the risks of spying were simply too great and the chances of enjoying any rewards too small. Soviets who might have turned to spying were more interested in getting out of the system than in staying inside the system while making money on the side by selling secrets.

Yet, despite the fact that the KGB won the spy war, the Soviet Union is history, and the world now has only one superpower, the United States of America. Good intelligence never guarantees victory, and bad intelligence doesn't necessarily ensure defeat. Knowing the enemy's secret plans won't do much good if his army is bigger, better equipped, better trained, better motivated, more combat ready, and holding the high ground.

Throughout the Cold War the KGB was playing catch-up. It did steal our atomic secrets, but by the time the Soviet Union had built its first atomic bomb we were already stockpiling hydrogen bombs. The Soviets got ahead of us just once, the launching of the first satellite, but even after Sputnik we quickly caught up, and we didn't have to steal any of their secrets to do it.

Soviet secrets were things we didn't have to know or things we already knew. Indeed, critics of the CIA insist that much of the money spent in attempting to recruit spies inside the Soviet government not only failed to get good intelligence information, but even if they had succeeded, what the CIA would have learned would not have been worth the money spent on collecting the intelligence.

Even when we did get good intelligence, it was often ignored because it suggested that the Soviet Union was not the dangerous monster our politicians tried to make it out to be, but rather a disastrous economic and social experiment that was doomed to failure, regardless of what we did to oppose it.

The Expected Results of Spying Must Justify the Costs

Anyone who decides to take up spying needs to ask the questions the U.S. intelligence community never asked itself before asking Congress for lots of money: what exactly does one expect to learn, and will the information be valuable enough to justify the cost and the potential risk?

In the case of Janet Thompson, the information on what her husband was planning was well worth the small cost and even the risk her brother took. But let's look at another example of private spying.

Jeffery Zweibel was the chief executive officer at Modern Fashions, which produced and sold economy-priced women's clothing that pretended to be high fashion. For several years Modern Fashions had run a close second in sales to Parisian Day. Zweibel was concerned that Parisian Day was starting to pull ahead in both sales and profits, even though both companies sold similar products at about the same price.

While attending a high school reunion, Jeffery met an old friend, Terry Daniels, whom he hadn't seen in 25 years. Daniels had just retired at age 50 from a government job in which he had worked overseas in a half-dozen different countries. As the two men renewed their friendship, Terry had little to say about what he did for the government. He was much more interested in listening to Jeffery talk about his business.

After Jeffery complained about how he was losing out to the competition, Terry suggested that Jeffery ought to do some spying on the opposition and learn what secrets might be responsible for Parisian Day's success. When Jeffery complained that he didn't have any idea how to launch such an effort, Terry offered to help Jeffery out, but warned his friend that a good intelligence collection effort would be expensive. When Jeffery asked how expensive, Terry began scribbling on a notepad as he worked out how much he would have to charge to recruit several spies inside Parisian Day. The proposed six-figure price staggered Jeffery, and he rejected the plan.

Four weeks later, one of Modern Fashions' biggest buyers announced that she was dropping the Modern Fashions line and would be buying exclusively from Parisian Day. Convinced that Parisian Day had done something dirty in excluding Modern Fashions from a major market, Jeffery called Terry and, out of desperation, agreed to the proposed terms for running a spying operation against Parisian Day.

Over the next several weeks, Terry, working with several service agents, successfully recruited five Parisian Day employees as spies.

The first recruit was Tonya Lopez, a cleaning lady. A middle-aged, single mother, Tonya had a 19-year-old son, Eduardo, who had recently been arrested and charged with aggravated assault following a street gang fight. While waiting in the courtroom for a hearing on the charges, Tonya met Imelda Melendez, a young woman who claimed to be working for one of the many advocacy groups that serve the city's poor. Imelda arranged for a lawyer, who got the charges against Eduardo reduced to a misdemeanor with no time in jail. (Tonya never noticed that Imelda helped only one person in a courtroom full of defendants.)

Several days later, Imelda told Tonya that the advocacy group she represented was investigating the abuses of workers in the garment industry. Using implied threats that Tonya's son could find himself back in court facing new felony charges, combined with the offer of regular cash payments, Imelda convinced Tonya that she should begin spying on her employer.

Tonya was soon passing on to Imelda the contents of the trash cans in the Parisian Day executive office. She also planted several different listening devices in such places as the CEO's office, her conference room, and the ladies' bathroom. Just as important, Tonya told Imelda a great deal of information about the people who worked at Parisian Day: their names, their positions, what kinds of private things they kept in their desks, the telephone numbers in their Rolodexes, descriptions of their cars and their license plate numbers.

David Misisco worked as a midlevel executive in the Parisian Day sales office. David was angry that a female colleague had gotten a promotion that he had wanted and was convinced that she had gotten the promotion only because of affirmative action. David complained bitterly about his situation to his new friend, Joe Killory, whom he met while taking a night course in salesmanship at a city college. A sympathetic Killory let it slip that he sometimes sold information and suggested that there were people who would pay good money for inside information on Parisian Day's sales campaigns. Although Killory wouldn't say who his customer might be, David assumed it was Modern Fashions. He happily agreed to become a spy inside Parisian Day. David not only enjoyed the money that Killory (really Daniels) started paying him, he also got a major kick out of playing spy with all the dead drops, secret meetings, and surveillance-evasion training that Daniels provided.

Regina Menes, who worked in the Parisian Day executive secretary pool, met Donald Snell at a church social and soon fell hopelessly in love. Snell, who told Regina he worked on Wall Street as an investor, promised to marry her as soon as he cashed in on several investments he had made based on insider information. Then one day Donald appeared at Regina's apartment, wearing a terrified expression and telling her that a stranger had approached him on the street and handed him an envelope containing evidence of his insider-trading activity. The blackmailer didn't want a monetary payoff to keep him from passing the information to the Security and Exchange Commission; he wanted Donald to convince Regina that she should begin spying on her bosses at Parisian Day.

At first Regina refused, but after several nasty lovers' spats, a threat of suicide, and a promise that she would only have to go along until Donald could cash in the trades and collect the profits, she met with a stranger (Terry Daniels, of course), who taught her how to pass him information through a dead drop.

Terry also succeeded in recruiting a delivery driver and one of the Parisian Day bookkeepers, Alan Stremple.

This was a casebook study in how to recruit and run a ring of spies. Each of the spies had been recruited under a different false flag, and none of them knew about the others.

Six months after putting Terry on the payroll, Jeffery knew all the secrets there were to know about Parisian Day. He had learned that Parisian Day was contracting out most of its sewing work to sweatshops that employed undocumented aliens, that its bookkeepers were cooking the books to avoid income taxes, and that it was stealing pattern designs from the more expensive fashion houses. These, however, were also things that Jeffery was doing at Modern Fashions.

Jeffery also had a foot-high file with the details of Parisian Day's production and sales procedures. He had the list of customers, the total sales figures, production costs, personal details on buyers, and just about everything else that someone at Parisian Day had written down over the last five years. He had drawings of Parisian Day's planned fashion designs, its distribution figures, and advance information on its advertising campaigns.

Jeffery also knew a lot about the people who worked at Parisian Day, including the CEO, Donna Sposato. He knew that Donna's current lover was Sharon Katzke, something that David didn't know. Jeffery also knew the current balance in Ms. Sposato's personal bank account, what medication she was taking, and where Donna and Sharon did their social drinking as well as the bed and breakfast where they often spent weekends. He had the same kind of personal information on every single executive working for Parisian Day.

Yet, despite the stacks of documents and reports from the spies he had working inside Parisian Day, Jeffery didn't have a single bit of actionable intelligence, that is, information he could use to gain an advantage over the competition.

The simple fact, which Jeffery refused to consider, was that while Modern Fashions and Parisian Day produced almost identical lines of clothing, Donna was a better manager and CEO than he was. Most people liked working for her, and they worked just a bit harder at Parisian Day than at Modern Fashions. This influenced the way that Parisian Day employees dealt with customers, who, as a result, liked Parisian Day sales and service personnel more than they liked those working for Modern Fashions. Therefore, if all other factors such as price, quality, and fashion design were equal, which they usually were, buyers would give as much business as they could to Parisian Day.

If Jeffery had bothered to ask just about anyone in the fashion industry why he was losing business to Parisian Day, they might have told him the truth. But he wasn't the kind of man who would ever admit to himself that anyone knew the fashion business better than he did.

Desperate to use the intelligence he had paid so much to obtain, Jeffery finally decided the best way to hurt Parisian Day would be to pass on the information he had on Parisian Day's tax avoidance to the IRS. He did so, and Parisian Day soon had a visit from IRS examiners that would eventually cost the company more than a hundred thousand dollars.

Even here, Parisian Day was served by its employees. The head of accounting quickly identified midlevel bookkeeper

Alan Stremple as the source of the information that had been passed to the IRS. Donna immediately fired Stremple, and her senior accountants were able to neutralize most of the damage he had done. Although Parisian Day did have to pay back taxes, the total amount was a great deal less than what the IRS officers had been led to expect they would collect.

An angry IRS supervisor then decided to look closely at other businesses in the garment industry, starting with the name he already knew. Jeffery did not have bookkeepers who were as clever or as loyal to the company as Parisian Day's. Jeffery's bills for back taxes, combined with his business losses, forced him into bankruptcy.

Avoiding Intelligence Mistakes

Jeffery's first mistake was forgetting the primary rule of business: keep your eye on the customer. What he should have asked was, "What is Parisian Day giving the customers that my company is not?" The people who had the answer to the question were the customers themselves. He needed some good, legitimate market research, not an espionage system managed by a washed-out CIA case officer.

Jeffery's real problem was self-deception. He refused to admit to himself that his declining sales and the loss of old customers were signals that he wasn't meeting the demand of the customers.

The moral of this story is simple: before deciding to spy on someone else, you must first have a very good idea about what information you expect to find, and you should have a clear plan on how you intend to use that information to gain an advantage. Too many people, including many in government, spy on others because they can't figure out what else to do. They begin by deceiving themselves, refusing to recognize their own failures to serve the legitimate needs of their customers or citizens. Instead, they hope to discover an explanation for their personal and institutional failures in the camp of an enemy.

Chapter Eleven

Surveillance

A successful spy-recruitment operation begins with successful surveillance. You should start a surveillance operation as soon as you decide to start spying on someone else. The question you need to answer before beginning surveillance is not how much surveillance should be done, but, rather, how much budget and manpower can be committed to surveillance, and how to use them most effectively to gather the most important information.

Because there are numerous good books describing the skills and techniques of surveillance, including several outstanding works in the Paladin catalog, I won't describe the details of surveillance techniques. Instead, I will focus on what a good intelligence case officer hopes to discover through surveillance. Nevertheless, the reader must understand that surveillance skills, including skills in the use of surveillance photography and high-tech listening devices, are extremely important for every intelligence case officer. Every professional intelligence-collection agency in the world puts its case officer trainees through long hours of rigorous instruction and practice in surveillance, surveillance avoidance, and spotting others who are watching or following the trainee.

The case officer watches the target organization's office

and everyone who works and visits there to identify employees and associates of the target. The surveillance must identify everyone who might be an important part of the organization, especially those who might know the secrets of the organization or have access to those who will know the secrets the case officer wants to steal.

Employees are easy to identify because they show up to work and leave at the end of the day at roughly the same times. Also, they can often be identified as to the type of work they do by what they wear to work. Professionals dress in suits; delivery men, cleaning women, and maintenance people dress more casually and may wear uniforms. Once the case officer identifies such people, then the surveillance expands to watching them. The surveillance must discover who they are, where they work, where they live, what they do in their spare time, and, most important, what they do that they want to keep secret. Cars, homes, and recreational activities will also provide considerable data on levels of income and how important each employee is to the target organization.

The most important goal of the preliminary surveillance is to identify possible recruits for spying—those who have access to intelligence and who might be conned into spying. Once potential recruits are identified, the surveillance should look closely at each potential recruit, trying to learn everything possible about their lives, especially uncovering personal problems or moral weaknesses. This will include evidence that a potential recruit lives above his income, has difficulty getting along with other people, has family problems, and any other information that might be used in a recruitment attempt.

LOOK AT WHAT THE SURVEILLANCE TARGET THROWS AWAY

It's amazing what some people throw away—canceled checks, old credit card receipts and their carbon copies, empty medicine bottles, personal letters, memos and reminder notes, old bills, grocery receipts, shopping lists, lottery and betting tickets, and sometimes things they never intended to throw away but accidentally dropped into a trash can. You can learn the addresses of friends and business contacts from envelopes, the type of medicine they are taking, all about their personal finances, what kind of legal problems they face, what unions or professional associations they belong to, where their children go to school, what magazines the family reads, how much they drink and so on.

Even though the public has been warned repeatedly about the dangers of throwing away such things as credit card charge copies and bank balance sheets, most people keep tossing such things in the trash and then putting out the trash where anyone can pick it up before the garbage collector comes along.

Government intelligence and police agencies understand the intelligence value of garbage; therefore, most government agencies with any security concerns burn all their paper trash. Most private citizens, public organizations, and business offices are notoriously lax about controlling trash that leaves the office and even more careless when it comes to disposing of written material while at home or on the road.

The most serious problems in collecting garbage are avoiding being observed while picking up the can and doing it in a way that the subject never realizes that his garbage is being examined by an adversary. A part of the ongoing surveillance should establish the household or office trash routine so that the garbage can be retrieved without being observed between the time it is placed in a Dumpster or set out for pickup and the time it is collected by the garbage truck.

IDENTIFY YOUR TARGET'S ENEMIES

Anyone who is engaged in a dispute of any kind with a target of an intelligence penetration is a potential source of information. Thorough surveillance can identify angry ex-lovers, fired employees, political opponents, business competitors, people owed money by the target, rivals for promotion, and anyone else who might wish harm to the target, his friends, and his employees. Such people will often know a lot about the one they hate and will willingly share the dirt with almost anyone who will listen to them.

LISTEN TO WHAT YOUR
TARGET IS SAYING

What is your target saying in public and in private conversations to which you are privy? If it's a business, read the annual reports and advertising copy. If it's a political organization, read the press releases and listen to what is put on the public record. Go to public meetings or send someone to such meetings. Look at credit reports, public tax records, documents required by campaign laws, court records, and every official, semiofficial, and public document you can lay your hands on.

WHAT WILL YOUR TARGET
TELL YOU IF YOU ASK?

The whole idea behind diplomacy is that both sides assume that it is a better idea to exchange information than it is to fight. Obviously, when two hostile parties talk, both sides will be telling lies about their intentions, their strengths, and their fears. Even so, the master of deception must also learn to be a master in recognizing deception in others. Sometimes, people telling lies let slip more truth than they realize. (Remember, a good lie must have a lot of truth mixed with it.) If you recognize the lie, then you can guess what truth the lie is trying to cover.

Oftentimes, face-to-face, nonthreatening confrontations will reveal more about your target than you can learn through a sophisticated spy program. This is especially true if you use the techniques of friendly interrogation as described in Chapter 8 when meeting with your enemy in person. Use such a meeting to learn as much about your enemy as you can while revealing only those things about yourself that will strengthen your position with the enemy.

IF POSSIBLE, GET AN INVITATION TO THE TARGET'S HOME

This is often easier than you would suppose, provided the intelligence officer or one of his agents is not known to the target. You might pretend to be a repairman, salesman, private investigator collecting information on a neighbor, volunteer for a charity soliciting donations, or even a policeman or fireman offering a free safety inspection.

Once inside a home, always have a sudden nature call. It's surprising how much you can learn about someone by gaining access to the bathroom and the medicine cabinet.

This is best demonstrated by a recent scam in which a tent preacher, who claimed he could heal the sick, would spy on believers who had written letters requesting free front seat tickets to one of his healing revivals. A few days before the revival, a well-dressed young woman driving a new model car would fake a mechanical breakdown in front of the target's home. The young woman would attempt to fix the car by working under the hood for a bit, making sure she got some dirt and grime on her hands. Then, acting frustrated and angry, she would ring the bell of the target's house and ask to use the phone, explaining that she was supposed to be at an important meeting and that she needed to call the people expecting her and then call an auto club. Once the calls were made, she asked if she could use the bathroom to wash the grease and grime off her hands.

In the bathroom, she would open the medicine cabinet. What she learned would be put to good use at the next revival meeting. On the night of the next revival, the preacher walked through the audience, proclaiming that God—through him, of course—was looking for someone to bless with a healing: "I see a woman named Evelyn who is chained to Valium. Dr. Bernheart writes her the prescription because he can't heal her like God can. The expensive vitamins that Evelyn buys from the Nature's Way Vitamin Company won't do it either. The double-strength aspirin she buys in the 200-tablet bottles helps the pain for only a while, but God wants to help her for eternity."

Evelyn, convinced that the preacher had a direct line to the Almighty, didn't think about the pretty young lady who asked to use the phone several days earlier as the preacher suddenly turned, looked at her, and asked, "Your name is Evelyn, isn't it?"

Once you know everything that can be learned through surveillance about the target and those who work for him or have some personal relationship with him, you are ready to start recruiting people to spy on the target.

Chapter Twelve

The Basic Steps: Phase One

There are seven basic steps in the recruitment and running of a covert spy, divided into two phases. The first three steps make up phase one, which we'll discuss in this chapter. The remaining four steps, phase two, will be detailed in Chapter 13.

Phase One
- Spotting
- Evaluation
- Recruiting

Phase Two
- Testing
- Training
- Handling
- Termination

SPOTTING

The major products of good surveillance will be a list of potential recruits for spying.

There are two primary criteria that must be considered in

identifying a potential recruit. The first criteria is that of access: does the potential recruit have access to the information the intelligence collector wants to steal? Potential recruits should be rated in order of the probability that they will have access to secret intelligence or have a personal relation with someone who has access.

The second criteria is personality assessment: is the potential recruit someone who can be subverted?

Anyone looking for a good spy should focus on the following classes of employees in the target organization:

- *Angry or desperate upper- and midlevel management personnel.* These are the people who have lost the trust of their colleagues or have personal secrets that would lose them such trust if their secrets were discovered. Stuck on the career ladder because of their own incompetence, they fear that they are going to lose their jobs and are looking for both sympathy and someone to blame for their failure to succeed. The best prospects are those who have been recently passed over for promotion. They will be angry and may be looking for possible revenge, a way out of the dilemma, or some way to remake their world into something more to their liking.
- *Clerks, secretaries, and communications personnel.* These people see lots of secret information. Although most such employees are surprisingly loyal to their bosses—despite their low position on the pay scale—many have personal problems and vices that make them potential subjects for recruiting. They may have tastes they can't afford to feed, and they are envious of those who can afford such luxuries, especially among their higher-paid colleagues.
- *Janitors, drivers, cleaning ladies, and other "invisible" people.* Underpaid and often ignored or even mistreated, these workers always need more money for the simplest things. Many of them have more access to secret information, or can get access, than the movers and shakers in the organization ever imagine.

The best potential spies for combining both criteria are the unglamorous and sometimes ugly people who in their often dull and always routine jobs have access to secrets.

Other especially good prospects are antisocial personalities incapable of loyalty to anything. These types of people are also the most likely to have secret vices. They may gamble when they don't have money to cover the losses, drink too much, use illegal drugs, engage in high-risk sexual behavior, and have domestic problems. Most important, they are looking for easy ways out of their troubles.

Unfortunately, life is no more fair for the intelligence case officer than it is for anyone else, and the best is not what you usually get. Instead of identifying the perfect recruit, most case officers find themselves with a list of potential recruits, none of whom come close to matching what the case officer hopes to find. The person with the best access to the information will be a recently promoted, contented worker, who is happily married with great kids, no serious vices, and a highly developed sense of loyalty.

Often, the initial surveillance will discover no one who might have access to valuable information and who fits the personality profile of a potential spy. Compromises must then be made, and the experienced case officer will usually choose the person with the personality traits that make him an easier target for recruitment over the person who has better access to information. It is better to have a less-than-adequate spy than no spy at all.

In such situations the case officer will have to settle for an initial recruitment of an access agent, someone who has direct access to others who may eventually prove to have potential as a primary agent. At the very least, a good access agent can provide the access necessary to plant electronic bugs, take pictures of physical plants, or report on officer gossip.

EVALUATION

Once the case officer has identified potential recruits, each one must be thoroughly evaluated in order to identify the possible motives for why the target would be induced to turn traitor and to determine what type of approach will most likely succeed. The case officer must then decide who will make the initial approach, what cover story the recruiting case officer will use, what enticements will be offered to cement their friendship and create anticipation for more rewards, and how the recruit will be managed through the recruitment process.

The case officer must also decide if he will attempt to use the target as an unintentional spy, or if the recruit will be manipulated into a position where he voluntarily agrees to spy, perhaps as a favor to his new friend or because the friend offers to solve the target's personal problems.

RECRUITING

The basic formula a case officer uses for recruiting a spy is a simple one.

- The case officer, or someone controlled by the case officer, pretends to be someone the target would respect, desire, admire, or perhaps even fear..
- The recruiter arranges to meet and get to know the target.
- Once acquainted, the recruiter develops a close personal relationship with the target based on one or more of the bonds of friendship, such as sexual attraction, common interests, similar personalities, common political objectives, or mutual hates, and offers to help solve personal problems.
- The recruiter builds the relationship into one in which the target trusts the recruiter and looks to him for advice and help in solving personal problems. At the same time, the recruiter will subtly encourage and support the behavior that creates those personal problems.

- The recruiter asks the target to do innocent favors and services and rewards the target with praise, money, sex, drugs, psychological support, or a combination of those things.
- Taking advantage of the growing trust and dependence of the target, the recruiter asks the target to provide unimportant bits of information about the organization targeted for intelligence collection. The recruiter treats such harmless bits of knowledge as more important than they really are and rewards the target for his service.
- As the target responds in a positive manner, the recruiter makes additional requests that step progressively closer to treason. The recruiter increases the rewards given to the point that the target comes to expect and, perhaps, becomes dependent on them. At the same time, the recruiter helps the target to find psychological justification for betraying those who trust him.
- The recruiter takes the final step, asking the target to provide important information that will be a clear betrayal of his earlier loyalties to his government, employer, trusted confederates, or lover.

Choosing the Recruiter

The case officer may either handle the initial contact himself or use a surrogate he controls. A surrogate recruiter can be an access agent, some third party who doesn't realize he is being used, or another case officer picked because he has the specific personality traits needed. It is also possible that a case officer from a different territory will be brought in to handle the recruitment in case the operation turns sour. In such an event, the recruiting officer can go home after the failure, and the primary case officer can look for another recruit, without having to fear exposure by the target of the failed attempt.

If another professional case officer is used, he should be fully informed about the reasons for recruitment and what the operations officer expects to get from the recruit. On the other hand, an access agent may know little or nothing about why the target is being recruited or, for that matter, who will really benefit from the spying.

Preferably, such an access agent will not know who he is really working for. For example, a case officer may hire a prostitute who approaches a potential recruit known to be ripe for a love experience. The case officer tells the prostitute that the target is a business customer he wants to get relaxed and ready to deal with when, in fact, the case officer is a KGB agent who wants to set up the target for a blackmail recruitment. The prostitute, at the instruction of the case officer, may then pretend to be a college student looking for work or a recently divorced woman looking for love when she meets the target for the first time.

Once the access agent gets to know the target and earns his love or trust, he will lead the target into an introduction with the case officer, who will then take over direct control of the target. For example, the prostitute might first develop a romantic relationship with the target and then introduce the target to the case officer at a social function as an old friend or relative. In other situations, the access agent or the contact case officer may introduce the primary case officer to the target during a chance meeting in a restaurant, on a golf course, at church, or in a bar.

It may be impossible to make direct contact with the best potential recruit. Perhaps he never goes out in public, or he hides behind a secretary who screens all his appointments and is extremely suspicious of any approach by a stranger who has not been properly introduced. In such a case, the case officer may enlist the help of an innocent third party who is close to the target, perhaps a relative, an old friend, a business associate, or even his wife or child. The case officer first makes friends with the associate or family member, and then when he gains that person's trust, he manipulates the unwitting accomplice into introducing the target to him.

Whether he makes the initial contact or uses a surrogate, the case officer arranges a meeting with the potential recruit that appears to be a normal occurrence in the daily life of the recruit. In most cases, it should take place in a nonthreatening social situation, preferably when the potential recruit is relaxing away from the office. The target might be approached while on vacation, at church, or perhaps traveling in a foreign country.

Government agencies often approach a target while he is traveling abroad. Indeed, if he lives in a repressive country in which the government regularly spies on its citizens, recruitment in a foreign country may be the only possibility. The Mossad almost never stations case agents inside Arab countries. Instead, they focus their recruitment efforts on Arabs who travel abroad.

The idea is to set up a social situation in which the target remembers the meeting as one in which *he* took the initiative. It is best if a situation is designed so that the target approaches the recruiter and introduces himself.

In one counterespionage operation targeted against an intelligence officer working in the Soviet Embassy, an FBI recruiting team began attending meetings of a technical society where the suspected Soviet case officer often hung out. One of the members of the FBI team always arrived alone and remained aloof from the other participants during the meetings, but occasionally asked probing questions that suggested that he was a highly qualified technical expert. The Soviet Embassy case officer, obviously curious, started asking other guests at the meeting about the stranger, but no one seemed to know anything about him. Eventually, the Soviet agent asked one member of the FBI recruitment team, who told the Soviet a cover story that identified the stranger as a scientist working for a government contractor in the missile industry— an obvious target for Soviet recruitment.

Soon, the Soviet agent approached the planted FBI agent, who artfully managed to turn the tables and recruit the Soviet to spy for the FBI. What started out as an attempt at recruiting an American to spy for the Soviets ended up in the successful recruitment of a Soviet intelligence office, who provided extremely valuable information for several years. (This particular spy became one of the first victims after Rick Ames started spying for the KGB. Ames exposed the man to the KGB, and he was then suddenly transferred back to the Soviet Union, arrested, and eventually executed.)

In some circumstances the intelligence team might want to create a situation in which the target, or a lover or family member of the target, is placed in danger, then the recruiter appears on the scene and rescues the target. Two support agents might attack a potential recruit on a dark street. As she is about to be raped, a passing motorist stops and scares the rapists away. The rescuer, pretending to be a good Samaritan, then takes the woman to a police station or wherever she wants to go.

Instead of being the primary target, the woman might be the daughter of the primary target. The heroic case officer then accepts an invitation to meet with the father who wants to extend his thanks.

Another ploy is to arrange a minor traffic accident that allows the opportunity to exchange names and addresses. The recruiter doesn't have to be in the other car; he could be the witness who got a description and license number of a hit-and-run driver.

The plot for such threatening situations might be rewritten so that it is the recruiter who appears to be in danger and the potential recruit saves the day. This works especially well if the initial contact agent is a pretty woman and the potential recruit scares off the criminals who are dragging her into an alley or are running away with her purse.

In a previous chapter we saw how a case agent first set up a love match, put the love in danger, and then introduced himself to the target, offering a solution that saved the girl and protected the target from exposure.

Wherever the initial approach is made, it should be a situation in which the case officer has control and can retreat quickly if something goes wrong. Although the recruiting operation should be carefully planned out in detail, the case officer must be ready to flow with the events and situations and be prepared to take advantage of sudden opportunities.

Throughout the recruitment process, intelligence officers should intensify the surveillance of the prospect. All meetings between the recruiter and subject should be monitored by a surveillance team. If possible, both sound and videotape recordings should be made. The intelligence team should gather any evidence that might be used to incriminate the subject—fingerprints, photos, tape recordings, and eyewitnesses—in the event the recruitment effort fails.

Once the target meets the case officer, the latter, who will almost always pretend to be something he is not, begins to build a nonthreatening friendship with the target. At the same time, everything the case officer says or does must be designed to put the target at ease and make him or her enjoy the new friendship; the case officer should do nothing that puts the target off guard about the possible dangers of such a friendship.

The case officer must do whatever is necessary to become a trusted friend on whom the prospective recruit believes he can rely. To do this, the case officer will do the following:

- Listen to the target talk
- Sympathize with the target's problems
- Offer easy solutions to the target's problems and lend a helping hand in solving such problems
- Feed the target's prejudices and play to his vanity, fears, and hopes
- Grant the target absolution (no matter what terrible things he admits to having done)
- Ask the target for simple favors and be grateful when they are granted but gracious when the target cannot help
- Never criticize what the target holds dear

As the friendship develops, the case officer or his controlled surrogate leads the target into spying by making it appear to be a natural outcome of the friendship. Often, the clever case officer will create a situation in which information becomes a commodity the target can use to help solve a problem faced by the target or the case officer himself.

The first request for information will be for something that appears to be harmless and perhaps even legitimate. It may be something as simple as a request for a company telephone book, training manual, or list of salesmen or company employees. The next step toward treason will be a request for something a bit more sensitive, but this time it will be accompanied by an offer of some kind of reward.

Gradually, the new friend leads the target into increasingly illegal and immoral behavior, all the while making it appear that the traitorous acts are further cementing the friendship or love affair. The inducement to treason may be psychological motivation, sex, money, or a combination of all three.

In some situations, the case officer may arrange secretly to create problems that threaten the target's peace of mind, employment, marriage, or even his life or the life of someone he loves. For example, a case officer may use an access agent to plant evidence that will get the target in trouble with his boss or the law. The case officer then sympathizes with the aggrieved employee or loyal citizen while subtly suggesting that the target owes no real loyalty to such an unfair employer or government.

If blackmail is used as an inducement to treason, the case officer will usually not be the one making the blackmail threat. A crude entrapment followed by blackmail threats from the case officer can easily backfire, and if it does, the case officer will have to withdraw and the recruitment effort abandoned. A clever case officer will arrange for someone else to make the blackmail approach, and then he will offer a way to get out of the blackmail situation or collect the funds necessary to pay the blackmail demands. The recruiter may even pretend to be another victim of the same blackmailer. This was the method used in the following example.

The Manila Blackmail Recruitment

The target of this recruitment operation, Carl Larson, was in Manila on a business trip when he overheard two Americans talking in a hotel bar about their home town of San José, California. Carl interrupted and introduced himself as someone who called San José home, too. The two men asked Carl to join them for a drink and introduced themselves as Bob French and Bill Lee.

Bob told Carl that he and Bill had just met and joked about what a long way the three had come to meet a couple of neighbors. The three men exchanged business cards, had a few more drinks, and then Bill, who had bragged about his frequent travel to the Philippines, suggested that he take the other two men on a tour of the infamous Manila night life.

After numerous drinks and stops at a half-dozen different girly bars featuring full nudity, the three men took three Filipino women they had met along the way to a short-time hotel that Bill recommended. There, the three men split company, and each took his date to a separate room.

The next morning, Carl woke up with a terrible hangover and a heavy load of guilt, compounded by the fear that the woman, who didn't look all that pretty or young in the morning light, might have given him something he didn't want to take home to his wife. Carl paid the lady and then took a taxi back to his hotel with a quick stop at a pharmacy where he bought enough antibiotics to ensure that he wouldn't come down with any of the less deadly diseases of love. He saw neither Bob nor Bill during the remainder of his stay in Manila.

Three weeks later, when he was back home in San José, Carl opened an envelope delivered by a messenger and discovered a videotaped recording of his activities with the Filipino prostitute. The accompanying note made the usual blackmail threats about sending copies to his wife, the press, and his employer unless Carl paid $50,000. There were also instructions for making the payment to a numbered bank account in Panama.

As Carl sat there, stunned and frightened, he received an angry phone call from Bob French, who accused Carl of setting him up for blackmail. French told Carl that because he was a bachelor and the owner of his own consulting company, he was blackmail proof. He not only refused to pay the blackmail, he threatened to go after both Carl and Bill Lee, who French was sure must have conspired to blackmail him. Carl, by now almost hysterical, vehemently denied the accusation and told Bob he was also being blackmailed—and that he wasn't blackmail-proof. Bob, cooling down, suggested that the two of them get together to discuss what to do next.

When they met, Bob started off by apologizing for accusing Carl of setting up the blackmail operation. He reported that since the morning conversation, he had tried to call Bill, but the number and address listed on Bill's business card were phony. Obviously, it had been Bill who set up both of them. Whereas Carl, who didn't have $50,000 in available cash, was terrified, Bob, although angry, apparently was not worried about himself. Bob pointed out that even if Carl found the money and paid it, that would just be the first installment. Going to the police wouldn't do any good either, because Bill was operating out of a foreign country.

Bob wanted to put the blackmailer out of business, permanently, and suggested that was Carl's best hope as well, provided that in the process they could get hold of the blackmail material. He told Carl he had some Philippine contacts he thought could do it for him, but he didn't want to make a move unless he knew that he had Carl's support. When Carl asked what that would cost, Bob told him not to worry, that his friends owed him a favor and that he felt partially responsible for Carl's problems because he hadn't spotted Bill for the blackmailer he was. Bob suggested that Carl keep his mouth shut and not pay any blackmail for the time being. The longer they discussed the action, the more Bob made it sound like he was going to solve the problem more as a favor to Carl than because of any concern about himself.

A week later, during which time Carl received two more letters demanding immediate payment, Bob called and suggested that the two of them meet for lunch. As soon as they had ordered the drinks, Bob explained that his contacts in Manila had found Bill's place of operation as well as evidence that he regularly enticed visiting Americans into blackmail situations. They also had learned that Lee kept his blackmail evidence in a safe in a small apartment where he lived in Manila. Bob's friends had it set up with a crooked Filipino police colonel to break into the apartment, open the safe, collect the evidence, and then "put Bill out of business, permanently."

There was just one hitch: the payoff to the police colonel for his help (to ensure that no one who engaged in the break-in would be caught and arrested) was going to cost more than either Bob or his friends had expected. Bob's friends in Manila had proposed a deal. They wanted a complete report on Carl's business activities during his visit to Manila, whom he met, what deals were arranged, and what kinds of profits Carl's company expected to make in Manila.

When Carl asked, Bob admitted that the information would go to a European competitor who wanted to make the deal with the Filipino corporation that Carl had been wooing. Bob added that his own opinion was that the competitor would get the deal anyway and that the Filipino firm had been stringing Carl's company along to use as leverage to get a better deal out of the European company.

In fact, Carl's trip to Manila had been a business bust. The proposed partner for the Filipino-American venture wanted too big a share of the stock, and unless the Filipino changed his mind and lowered his demands, there would be no deal, even without another competitor bidding for the business. Because Carl didn't want to go back to Manila ever again, he could have cared less if his company lost the market in the Philippines. He quickly agreed to do what Bob asked. A day later he gave Bob all the information he had requested.

A week later, Bob met with Carl again and handed him a

package containing the original negatives and videotape of Carl's Manila night. Bob also assured Carl that he didn't have to worry about Bill, who had "disappeared."

Bob had another surprise for Carl. His friends in Manila had found the information that Carl had provided so useful that they were paying a bonus. Bob then handed Carl an envelope containing $1,000. He asked that Carl sign a receipt for the money so Bob could prove to his friends that he had passed it on to the intended party. Bob assured Carl that no further record would be made of the transaction and that he could consider the money tax-free income that neither Carl's employer nor the IRS would ever know about.

As soon as he signed that receipt, Carl was hooked. The next time, Bob asked for a bit of commercial intelligence on Carl's company's plans for a pending deal in Singapore, Carl made $1,500, exactly what he needed to pay for the unexpected orthodontic work his daughter required. During the next several years, Carl passed increasingly sensitive intelligence about his company's overseas deals on to the man he knew as Bob French.

Bob and Bill had worked together in setting up the recruitment that entrapped Carl into becoming a corporate spy. Bill's disappearance wasn't murder; he just dropped the fake identity he'd used for one operation.

When the Case Officer Can Openly Blackmail the Recruit

Although the case officer is usually not the one who actually blackmails the recruit during the initial process, once the recruit is working as a spy, the case officer may use blackmail, if necessary, to keep the spy in line. The case officer should always collect the necessary evidence that he can use to blackmail a recruit who decides he doesn't want to spy any longer.

In the previous example, for as long as Bob controlled Carl, he kept in a safe his own copies of the photos and tapes of

Carl's night on the town along with the growing pile of receipts for the money he paid Carl for company secrets. But he never had to use that material to control Carl.

Creativity Is Always the Order of the Day

There are an infinite number of ways in which a case officer can deceive a target into turning traitor. The best method is one specifically designed to fit the emotional, psychological, and monetary needs of the target while subtly offering the target a justification for what he is going to do—steal information and give it to the new friend, who has suddenly become an important part of his life.

Sometimes, honesty—or better said, *some* honesty—is the best policy in a recruitment effort. If surveillance and investigation uncover that a potential recruit is already angry at his boss, he might jump at the chance to do a little spying for the competition, especially if he can make money doing it. Intelligence experts who engage in commercial espionage are always on the lookout for disgruntled employees who are looking for new employment.

In such a case, the direct approach, in which the case officer offers both immediate rewards and the possibility of future employment, may be the easiest, quickest route to recruitment. That's why the cold pitch described in Chapter 9 to recruit Silvestre Martinez worked. Martinez was in a career bind and he knew it, and he also knew that the only intelligence agency that would be interested in the information he had to sell was the CIA. When you have a potential recruit who will jump at the chance to work for the CIA, IRS, or FBI, or a business competitor who wants to put a recruit's mean boss out of business, a false flag is not only unnecessary, it may actually get in the way of recruitment.

However, even in those cases in which the case officer honestly admits what organization or agency he represents, some deception is still in order. The smart case officer will not use his real identity or give the recruit any information that would allow the recruit to identify him or learn anything about his personal life. It's always possible that the potential spy who appears so anxious to start spying for the case officer is, in fact, the bait set as a trap. It's also possible that the potential recruit will suddenly change his mind. In any case, the less that the recruit knows about the real person doing the recruiting, the better.

When the Recruitment Fails

There are no guarantees in life, and even the best-laid plans sometimes end disastrously. The recruit may recognize what is happening and immediately react to protect himself and those to whom he owes his loyalty. The target may break off contact, or he may go to his security officer, counterintelligence people, or the police. The worst-case scenario is one in which he continues to lead the recruiting case officer on, either to entrap him or to feed him false information.

The possibility that the target will be doubled in an attempt to spread disinformation is the reason why close surveillance of the target should continue throughout the recruitment effort. If the potential recruit starts meeting secretly with other people, the recruiting officer must be among the first to know.

Failed, aborted, and doubled recruitments always pose a serious threat to the intelligence agency, the private intelligence case officer, or the private citizen who initiates an espionage operation. Therefore, recruitment plans must always include procedures to follow in the event of failure or even betrayal. The espionage officer must assume that the subject who rejects a recruitment attempt will report the attempt to his government, employer, or agency.

As soon as there is good reason to believe that the attempt at recruitment has failed, or will fail, the case officer and any others engaged in the recruitment must break off all contact with the subject. Any contact points, such as office phone numbers or safe houses, must be shut down. The target must have no way to contact anyone associated with the recruitment once the recruitment effort is abandoned. This is why it is so important to use a false identity when recruiting, even when the recruiter is honest about what government or organization the spy will be serving. Those responsible for espionage activity must be able to make a credible denial if the target goes public or attempts to make a criminal charge.

If future attempts are made to recruit new subjects in the same target organization, the case officer must assume the target officers will be warned. The same false flag or cover story should not be used, and the same case officer should not attempt to contact another potential source in that target organization. This is why the CIA and other spy agencies often temporarily bring in a case officer assigned in another country for some extra duty whenever they initiate a recruitment. If the recruitment fails, the exposed case officer can immediately leave the country, and there will be no chance that the sour recruit will bump into the failed recruiter accidentally while walking through a shopping mall.

A clever recruitment effort using a false flag may cause the enemy problems even when it fails by spreading misinformation. Say, for example, a KGB case officer pretends to be an American interested in a relationship in order to recruit a young but homely woman working in a French atomic weapons production facility. When the woman's new lover starts asking questions about weapon production, she goes to her security officer like she is supposed to. The French counterintelligence agency attempts to trap the case officer, but he spots the tail on the target recruit and disappears forever. The French government then commits a great deal of time and effort trying to discover why the Americans are recruiting spies within the French nuclear production industry.

In a similar example from the world of private espionage, a case officer working for a large corporation attempted to recruit a spy inside a competitor's bookkeeping department by claiming to be working for the IRS and offering a sizable reward for the information he wanted the target to steal. The honest employee instead told his boss about the attempt to recruit him. The boss was no longer such a threatening competitor because he was worried too much about a possible government investigation into his financial affairs.

Whenever abandoning a recruiting effort, the case officer should do everything possible to embarrass or discredit the uncooperative target. He should expose any blackmail material, tell the failed recruit's wife about the girlfriend, anonymously report crimes to local police, and so on. The more trouble the failed recruit suddenly discovers in his life, the less likely he will be to spend time and effort trying to identify the man or woman who tried to turn him into a spy. If a case officer can't recruit an enemy's loyal employee to spy for him, he can make sure that the employee isn't the happy worker he once was.

Chapter Thirteen

The Basic Steps: Phase Two

E very new spy must be tested as soon as he starts passing intelligence to the case officer to make sure that the spy is delivering reliable information.

TESTING THE RECRUIT

The testing will continue for as long as the recruited spy provides intelligence information. The best way to test the new spy's reliability is to check his information against known facts. To do this, the case officer tasks the spy with finding out specific information without letting him know that the case officer already has that information.

For example, the CIA may already have identified a missile site by surveillance photography. So the case officer asks the new spy to steal a list of missile sites and then checks to make sure the known site is on the list provided by the spy. If what the spy provides doesn't jibe with what the case officer knows to be true, the new agent may be a liar, a plant, or just a poor source of information. Regardless of the reason for his inaccuracy, he is not credible, and if the situation cannot be corrected through threats or the termination of promised rewards, the spy should be dropped as a source.

Although stolen information can almost always be verified during the early service of the recruited spy, as the spy provides more sensitive and unique information, it will be more difficult to test information provided by the agent against other reliable sources.

If possible, any espionage operation should recruit more than one spy inside the target organization. By operating a ring of spies, the case officer can check each spy's information against the information provided by other spies. Each spy should have no clue about which of his colleagues is also spying for the enemy. It's best to recruit different spies under different false flags using different case officers as the control for each spy.

Eventually, the best and most useful spy may be providing intelligence information that is not available from any other source. This is the very reason why someone sets out to recruit a spy—to learn something that cannot be learned any other way. On the other hand, such single source information can be extremely dangerous if it's misinformation.

Sometimes the information can be easily verified by the results. For example, the spy reports that the enemy will attack Cartagena on Tuesday, and the enemy does just that. However, careful records must be kept of all information provided by the spy, and these must be checked against future events and other sources of information.

A rigorous scientific method must be followed in checking on the veracity of the information provided. If the information is indeed true, then all predictions of future events based on the stolen information will prove true. Even one prediction based on an agent's information that doesn't check out must raise serious doubts about the reliability of the agent. However, sometimes false predictions can be explained: "The prime minister changed his mind at the last minute and canceled the attack on Cartagena because he discovered that the enemy had been alerted to the attack." Often, when an intelligence report proves false, the excuses offered by the spy can be checked out. If the explanation cannot be verified, the intelligence operations officer must exercise even greater care in testing future information the agent provides.

In all intelligence-collection efforts that rely on recruited spies, lying is a constant consideration. In one case in the 1950s, the CIA paid millions of dollars to a Chinese agent who claimed he was running a network of spies that he had recruited inside China. He claimed his agents were reporting on social conditions, anti-government activities, and economic developments. The agents inside China supposedly delivered their reports to the U.S. agent by secret correspondence and radio transmissions.

In fact, the self-described private intelligence entrepreneur was lying. He based his reports on newspaper stories, public government documents, and propaganda broadcasts, all of which he collected outside mainland China. He had no ring of spies, no clandestine radio net, and no sources inside the People's Republic of China.

Because he was using many of the same sources that the CIA was—interception of radio and TV news programs and newspaper clipping services—the bogus spy's information generally tracked with what the CIA analysts already knew about Red China. By the time the CIA discovered the nature of the information, the agency faced a massive task in cleaning out the thousands of files based on the faked information provided by the bogus spy. The "spy" disappeared—along with the millions he had collected—and was never heard from again. Even worse, there is good evidence that the spy was working for the Republic of China in Taiwan; that is, he was telling U.S. intelligence what the Nationalist Chinese wanted the Americans to believe.

The fact that some information does check out is not irrefutable evidence that the source is reliable. Disinformation operations, such as when a spy is doubled and then used to pass false information to an enemy, always include factual information as a cover for the misinformation.

The three most dangerous mistakes an intelligence officer can make are as follows:

- To continue to accept unverified intelligence provided by a recruited spy after a piece of information has been proven false. (This is especially dangerous if previous information from the source made the intelligence officer look good with his superiors.)
- To refuse to accept information provided by a reliable agent—one whose previous information has always checked out—because the new information doesn't fit the officer's beliefs about what the enemy is doing or planning.
- To pressure the spy to provide intelligence that will verify the officer's unsubstantiated conclusions, which will likely just tempt the spy to create false intelligence to keep the payments coming in. (The worst sin a case officer can commit is to offer a spy a bonus if he produces intelligence confirming his own favorite theory. Never give a spy a reason to lie to keep the case officer happy.)

The whole purpose of spying is to learn information that changes our understanding of what the enemy is planning and will likely do.

WHEN INDEPENDENT
VERIFICATION ISN'T POSSIBLE

All too often, it's impossible to verify information independently before deciding what action to take based on that information. Sometimes intelligence collection evolves to the point that there is no way to verify a report, but if that information is acted upon, and it proves true, victory is guaranteed;. but if it proves false, disaster ensues. This dilemma is why so many intelligence agencies have turned to the polygraph examination as a way of testing recruited spies.

Fluttering the Recruit

The CIA and other government spy agencies often include the polygraph as one part of their testing process. The recruit will usually only submit to a polygraph examination after the recruiting process is completed and he realizes that he is indeed spying on his own government, employer, or friends. Once he realizes his predicament, however, the spy usually has no choice other than agreeing to be fluttered, provided the case officer can arrange a way to set it up. (The spy who is being paid to supply secrets and refuses to be fluttered is most likely lying.)

Some polygraph experts, the honest ones, will admit that the polygraph is really a psychological tool rather than a machine that measures truth. Anyone who understands what a polygraph will or will not do can often beat the machine. It doesn't work much better than a coin flip as a lie detector for many people, including those who have the most experience telling lies. When the machine does work, it works as often as not because the subject doesn't dare tell a lie out of fear that the machine will catch him.

There are several books that describe techniques on how to beat the machine, and many intelligence agencies instruct their employees and sometimes even their agents on these techniques. Rick Ames passed two polygraph tests while he was making millions of dollars selling out U.S. spies to the KGB.

Polygraph examinations are expensive; they require trained personnel, and the recruit must go to some secret location, such as a safe house, or even take a trip to another country so he can be fluttered. Even so, if the case officer has the means of fluttering a recruit, it is worthwhile doing so, as long as the case officer understands that the polygraph examination is one part of the drama of recruiting and evaluating the source, a scenario designed to make the recruit believe that his lies will be discovered and he will be punished.

This drama can affect a recruit so much that a private intelligence operator may want to arrange a fake polygraph examination if he doesn't have the budget and trained personnel for the real thing. Most people have never seen a polygraph machine, so it's a simple exercise to set up something that looks like a polygraph session does on television, hook up the subject, and let someone ask him a bunch of questions. In such a con it is surprising how often the subject will tell the truth because he thinks he can't lie without getting caught, or he will get so nervous that an interrogator won't need a lie detector to spot the lies he tells.

What the intelligence officer should never do is accept the word of the recruit based on the supposed results of a polygraph examination. The truth can only be determined by examining whether the information provided proves true. If not, then the recruit was lying or someone lied to him, no matter what the machine told the polygraph examiner.

Verification by Friendly Interrogation

Intelligence officers who understand the fallacy of depending on the polygraph rely more on the techniques of friendly interrogation to test their recruits. Each time a case officer meets with a recruit in a situation that permits a frank exchange of information, he interrogates the recruit in great detail about his collection of intelligence information.

When a friendly interrogation is done right, the subject may not even realize that he is being interrogated, but instead conclude that the conversation demonstrates the case officer's interest in and concern about the subject's daily activities and the risks he is taking by spying.

A good source-verification interrogation will take several hours (or even several days), with the case officer (or better, a trained interrogation officer) encouraging the recruit to talk about anything and everything dealing with his daily life and his spy activities.

If at all possible, the entire conversation should be recorded without the spy's knowledge. It's even better if the interview can be secretly videotaped. The more detail the recruit provides in answering questions, the better. The case officer wants to learn such things as to whom the recruit has been talking, the dates and time of day such meetings took place, where the meetings took place, who else attended, and what they ate. Every question should be asked in several different ways, but they should interspersed throughout the dialogue and not be sequential.

After such an interrogation, the case officer, the interrogator, and the support intelligence staff must go over the entire conversation, word for word, looking for possible contradictions and making specific comparisons with the answers to the same question asked in different ways.

Telling lies is a lot harder than telling the truth, and only the cleverest of deceivers can remember all the details necessary to make a lie hold together over a long interrogation. Most liars don't plan a story thoroughly, so they must create the details on the fly, which makes it even harder to remember the little lie they told two days ago. Most often it will be the little details that alert the case officer that the recruit is lying.

Perhaps the recruit describes a visit to a nuclear plant, and when asked a question about the weather, he reports it was a sunny day. When the case officer checks a weather report, he discovers that the day was heavily overcast. Maybe the recruit mentions that one of his sources was drinking a martini during one meeting. When the friendly interrogator asks several hours later what drinks were served at the meeting, the recruit, who has already forgotten what he said earlier, reports that everyone was drinking scotch.

Give a suspected liar a chance to talk, act as if you believe every word he says, and ask lots of questions. Sooner or later the liar will trip himself up.

TRAINING THE RECRUIT

Every recruit will eventually require some training in the craft of spying—such things as the use of miniature and spe-

cialized cameras, coded writing, computer encryption programs, radio transmissions, surveillance-detection techniques,
dead drops, and escape and evasion tactics. How much training is necessary will depend on the sophistication of the targeted organization, how the spy is collecting the information
he steals, and what personal experience and technical information he brings to the table when he agrees to spy.

Obviously, if the recruited spy is an employee of another spy agency, he will need to exercise extreme caution in
avoiding the counterintelligence security apparatus that
routinely searches for evidence of treason among its own
employees. On the other hand, the secretary recruited to
spy on a small business executive may have little reason to
fear exposure and thus need only minimal instruction on
the practical aspects of spying.

The training may range from no more than a couple of
hours of instruction in a safe house to an extended trip to a
neutral third country with long days of specialized instruction.
Training also provides opportunity to cement the relationship
between the recruited agent and the control apparatus, to
tempt the recruit with future rewards, and to make him feel
like he now belongs to a close-knit organization that will protect him in the event things go wrong.

Special emphasis should be given in the training session on
the techniques used to pass both instructions to the spy and the
intelligence collected by the recruited spy back to the case officer.

Arrangements should also be made for handling payments, and the training officer must emphasize the need for
discretion in how the money earned from spying is spent. The
training session should address the question of how to explain
sudden wealth—or, better, how to hide it. Rick Ames told his
colleagues in the CIA that he had married a Colombian
woman who had inherited a great deal of money from her
father. (The truth was that Rick's father-in-law left no wealth
when he died and Rick spent a good share of his income from
spying on the support of the mother-in-law in Colombia.)

Often, people who are recruited as spies discover they enjoy the secrecy and the excitement of showing up others, especially those whom they think have underestimated their abilities or taken advantage of them. Good case officers play on this. There may well be no need for secret drops, complicated plans for spotting surveillance, or secret passwords, but dramatics in both the training and use of such skills on a regular basis will serve to keep the recruited spy interested in the game.

THE PSYCHOLOGICAL HANDLING
OF A RECRUITED SPY

Eventually, the recruit will realize that he is spying on those who trust him. At this point, the surrogate recruiter should pass full control of the recruit to the case officer, if that has not already been done. This passing of control should appear to be a natural result of the recruitment process. In most cases, the recruiter should set up a meeting with the person who will serve as the regular case officer. "This is my uncle, who is going to help us solve our problem," or "This is the man I told you about, the one who will be paying you from now on." If the recruit has a dependent relationship with the original recruiter, especially if it involves a sexual relationship, the case officer may want to keep that relationship alive, at least for a short period or until the case officer can manipulate the recruit into a new dependency on the case officer.

At some point, the case officer should guarantee the safety of the recruit and his family. It is not important whether the guarantee is valid; what is important is that the recruit believes the guarantees is valid. (A good case officer will engage in any deception—no matter how cruel or false it may be—if the deception ensures the cooperation of the recruit.) The more convinced the recruit is that his spying will not result in personal tragedy for himself or his family, *if he does what the case officer demands*, the better spy he will be. (There is nothing wrong with letting the spy believe that if he fails to do what the case officer demands, he will be nostril-deep in rising water.)

Each recruited agent requires personal handling. The spy may want a buddy, a confessor, a mother, a leader, a lover, or a general. At the same time, the case officer must keep his own emotions under tight control at all times and never allow himself to develop any kind of emotional attachment to the recruit. The case officer has to play the great friend and buddy while mentally building a wall that will allow him to use the recruit in an effective manner without worrying about the consequences, even if that requires placing the recruit in extreme danger. Yet, he must keep the recruit from ever recognizing that he is being exploited in the most cynical manner.

The case officer should watch for signs of stress and be ready to reassure the recruit whenever necessary. Praise can be very important, especially for those who become spies for ideological reasons. The CIA made Oleg Penkovsky a secret U.S. citizen and a colonel in the U.S. Army. The KGB made John Walker an admiral in the Soviet navy, even though Walker's motivation for spying was pure greed.

At some point money almost always becomes a part of the equation. Paying a recruit works both as a reward and as a means of control, but determining how much to pay him can be tricky. The pay isn't based on what the information is really worth, but rather what the recruit can absorb into his lifestyle without making it obvious he has a new source of income. No case officer wants a recruit's sudden wealth to tip off his boss that the employee may be working for someone else. The money should be enough to be an important source of new luxury in the recruit's life, but not so much that it draws the attention of his friends, relatives, and colleagues.

If at all possible, the case officer should get a signature on receipts for any money passed to the recruit in payment for information. (The case officer can always blame the necessity for a receipt on superiors who don't trust him.) Such evidence can later be used to threaten an agent who wants to back out of his agreement to spy. Once a person has turned traitor, he should always fear the possibility that the control officer will betray him if he doesn't meet the demands the control officer makes.

Payments don't have to be made directly to the recruit. Phillip Agee reports that in Mexico, the CIA supported the mistresses of government officials, paying for their rent, automobiles, and shopping bills. The advantages of such a deal are obvious. There is no paper money trail leading directly to the recruit. He gets the luxuries he wants without having to worry about hiding a rich bank account. In a similar way, a case officer might pay off gambling debts, provide vacation accommodations, pay for airline tickets, cover the expenses of a nursing home for a recruit's mother, or buy property in a foreign country and register it in the recruit's name.

Once recruited, a spy may continue providing intelligence material for many years. Every intelligence agency has employees who follow career paths that will eventually result in promotions and transfers. That means that a case officer in most intelligence-collection operations will sooner or later have to transfer the spies he has been running to a new case officer.

Such a change of case officers presents special problems. Oftentimes, the agent will have developed a deep emotional attachment to the case officer and won't like the idea that he is being handed off to some stranger.

The original case officer is responsible for preparing the recruit for his new handler. He should offer credible explanations about why he can no longer handle the agent, explanations that fit under the false flag the case officer has been using. The old case officer must brief the new case officer on everything there is to know about the spies he will be inheriting.

Sometimes even the best preparation work won't make the recruit feel comfortable with his new control officer. Also, it sometimes happens that the recruit no longer wants to continue spying and will look at the change of handlers as his chance to break loose. In this situation, signed receipts, bank account records, photographic evidence of meetings, and recorded conversations can be very important. All spies are subject to the ultimate form of blackmail: the knowledge that they can be exposed to those they have betrayed.

Even when a case officer must openly threaten a spy to keep him producing, the case officer should try to shift the blame to some third party. "I'd let you go, but I'm in the same fix you are. The people who control me won't let either of us go. Neither of us has any choice, unless we are willing to go to jail, or suffer something worse."

TERMINATION

All things come to an end, and every recruitment plan should include plans for terminating the arrangement with the spy. The successful case officer will always be the one who decides that the relationship with a spy should end. Spies don't get to quit on their own. Even so, when a control officer decides to cut a spy loose, it goes much more smoothly if the spy can be convinced that the decision was mutual or even his own. That is easy to arrange if the spy wanted out but didn't dare because of fear of what the case officer would do if he tried to quit.

It gets more difficult when the spy enjoys what he is doing and the money he is making. Agents recruited under false flags can usually be terminated with less trouble than agents who know the true identity of those for whom they are working. The case officer who terminates an agent recruited under a false flag must make sure that he will not run into the agent in a public place in a situation in which the agent can learn who the case officer really is. This will be easier to do if the case officer knows a good deal about the terminated agent—his life-style, the place he works, and where he hangs out in his free time. If the case officer should accidentally meet the terminated agent on the street or somewhere else, he must be ready to instantly assume the false-flag role he played when he was running the agent. The longer a case officer works in any given area, the more likely such an accidental exposure becomes. This is one reason why most international spy agencies rotate their agents into new territories every two to four years.

The case officer should make the termination as easy as possible. He should not say anything critical of the agent's work, even if he knows the agent has been making up his intelligence. Instead, he should offer excuses that blame someone up the line in the intelligence agency, budget problems, or even the case officer's own career problems.

Whether it is a false-flag recruitment or the recruited agent knows who he is spying for, if the spy was motivated by greed, he won't be happy with the sudden loss of income and may even try to fake more important intelligence to keep the money coming in. When possible, the case officer should pay the terminated agent some kind of lump sum to ease the blow. If the case officer has a file of evidence that the recruit wouldn't want the people he has been spying on to know about, the case officer can make a few veiled threats at the same time he makes the payoff. It works best if the spy is told how long he will be spying at the outset and what kind of severance he will be paid when his services are no longer needed.

If the expectation is that the recruit will only be spying for a short time, perhaps only several weeks, then it's best to include an offer of a substantial bonus at the time of recruitment to be paid once the spy has completed the work.

International spy agencies often employ agents for many years, especially those recruited as access and supply agents. The CIA offers such agents retirement benefits and sometimes even an opportunity to immigrate to the United States for their retirement years. Government case agents usually offer the same kinds of benefits to primary agents who are engaged in the direct collection of intelligence under high-risk circumstances, especially those who become moles. Unfortunately, few such agents have ever lived long enough to collect their promised retirement benefits.

The worst kind of termination is when the recruit is caught spying. When that happens, the primary consideration of the case officer must be to protect himself and the intelligence agency that employs him. The case officer should only attempt to rescue the spy if he can do so without risking his own operational safety. In many cases, the case officer provides the spy an escape plan that he can use if he learns he is about to be arrested. But almost any escape plan must be initiated before the spy is arrested. Even then, the discovered spy will be on his own during the initial flight, at least until he crosses a frontier or makes it to a safe house controlled by the case officer.

If the recruitment is done under a false flag, it's quite likely that any escape plans previously discussed with the recruit will include promises that cannot be fulfilled. There was no way that Rashid Yasin could have ever arranged for the Silvermans to immigrate to Israel (see Chapter 6).

Nevertheless, even when a recruitment is done under a false flag, it is much better if the recruit can avoid capture and prosecution. Yasin probably did have a bundle of cash and false documents ready to give Irvin Silverman, along with some suggestions on how they could hide out until "I can arrange transportation to Israel." Unfortunately for the Silvermans, things fell apart too quickly, and Yasin had to save his own skin.

If a spy recruited under a false flag is captured, every member of the intelligence team should break off all contact with him. All offices, telephone numbers, safe houses, drops, and message centers should be immediately closed down, and any evidence pointing to the true identity of the recruiter or any of his agents should be cleaned up and destroyed.

Remember, the whole purpose of recruiting a spy is to steal information that the enemy doesn't know you have. Every termination should be designed to ensure that the theft of the intelligence remains a secret. If that can't be achieved, then the goal is to make sure that the case officer is not identified and captured.

Chapter Fourteen

The Security Aspect

Once a case officer has recruited a spy, he must take every possible precaution to ensure that the people who are the target of the intelligence collection do not learn that they have a spy in their midst. He must also make sure that should the target's counterespionage officers discover that there might be a spy in the organization, they cannot trace the spy back to the case officer or even verify his existence.

THE THREE STEPS TO SECURITY

The case officer must set up procedures for handling the spy that accomplish the following objectives:

- Establish security procedures that the recruit will follow to avoid attracting attention to himself as he steals information
- Establish secure methods of communication between the case officer and the spy
- Reduce personal contacts between the case officer and the spy to the absolute minimum required to maintain discipline, morale, and operational technique

ESTABLISHING SECURITY PROCEDURES

Most recruits solicit advice from their case officers on how to go about collecting intelligence without getting caught. If at all possible, the case officer should not simply recommend security procedures for the recruit but also arrange training for him in methods to avoid detection consistent with the security threat under which he will operate.

The Basics of Stealing Secrets

The safest method for stealing secrets is one in which the spy participates in or eavesdrops on conversations during the course of his legitimate workday, or in his ordinary associations with the targets of the intelligence operation. The spy may attend meetings where intelligence information is discussed, regularly overhear conversations near the desk where he works, or type up secret reports for the boss. In addition to what he hears and sees, the spy on the inside will have regular access to documents containing sensitive information. He might hold such documents in his private office during work hours and perhaps even in an office safe. He may even take documents home to work on.

This is low-risk spying because the spy is doing his job or playing the role that the source expects him to play. This is why Rick Ames was such a dangerous spy. He went to work every day and did exactly what he was supposed to do—and then told the KGB what it was that he had done and learned while on the job. The better such a spy plays the role of the loyal, hardworking (but not particularly ambitious) employee, or the grand but not demanding lover, the more he becomes the invisible person who makes a perfect spy.

Alternatively, the spy who has a close or intimate relationship with a primary source of information—perhaps a mistress or a lover—will get information by listening to the source brag about his work or by eavesdropping and going through documents the source leaves lying around.

The risks of discovery increase when the spy must eavesdrop on conversations he is not supposed to hear, such as a secretary listening in on phone conversations or a chauffeur rewiring a connection so that he can listen to conversations in the backseat (even when the passengers have turned off the intercom). This risky but often necessary behavior includes deliberately gaining access to documents the spy would not normally see in the course of a workday. A secretary might read documents on the boss' desk while he's in the bathroom, a file clerk might search through file cabinets that belong to an officer, or a chauffeur might open a briefcase left on the backseat while the employer goes to a meeting.

These kinds of spies will need the most advice from their control officers, not just on how to steal secrets, but also on how to keep their activities hidden, how to protect what they have stolen from discovery, and how to deliver such material safely to the control officer.

In such situations the spy should never steal documents, but should instead copy them or photograph them. If that is impossible, the spy should read the documents and write a summary from memory as quickly as possible.

The spy should also always have a story ready that explains why he accidentally overheard a conversation or saw a document. "I'm sorry, I didn't realize you were on the line. I was going to call Nancy in security and suggest we do lunch." If caught looking through papers on the boss' desk, a secretary might say, "I'm looking for the budget proposal. Did you pick it up?" Any inane explanation is better than no explanation, provided it is given without hesitation.

Remembering What You Have Learned

The spy doesn't just have to worry about getting caught while eavesdropping or reading a document he is unable to photocopy. He must also remember what he has heard or seen, sometimes for up to several hours, before he can find an opportunity to write the details down. Therefore, it is critical for the spy to develop the ability to memorize large quantities of information.

Memorization is a talent that can and, indeed, must be practiced. Good spies must develop good memories, and it's the responsibility of the case officer to encourage and help them to do so. Exercises in memorization techniques should be included in any training provided to the spy. Here's a simple memorization exercise.

Watch and videotape a television news broadcast, political debate, or a serious discussion of any kind. Wait 30 minutes, then write out a detailed report of everything you can remember. Include descriptions of the people who spoke, backgrounds, and any action observed, including unintended subconscious actions (like someone brushing back a loose strand of hair). Replay the tape several times noting all the things you missed in your original report. Do the same thing with additional programs over and over until your memory improves.

As soon as he is alone and can safely do so, the spy should write out complete, detailed summaries of any relevant conversations or documents. Perhaps the best way to do this is to dictate into a tape recorder and then write out the report, making the necessary changes as his memory is enhanced by the recording.

If there is any chance that such notes might be discovered, the spy should use some kind of "invisible" or coded writing. This can range from such old standbys as lemon juice, which is then exposed to heat to make it appear, to a variety of invisible inks that are commercially available.

Recording Conversations and Copying Documents

Obviously, it's better if the spy can record a conversation or make a copy of a document. This is a much higher-risk situation than eavesdropping or sneaking a peek. If someone is caught taking pictures of documents at work or wearing a wire to a confidential meeting, there is no story in the world that will convince the security officer that the suspect is engaging in an innocent activity. Indeed, most government agencies that handle classified information prohibit employees from taking personal cameras to their office. Even so, it's easy to learn to use a miniature camera; there are a number of such cameras on the market, and every case officer should supply such a camera to his recruits along with instructions on its use. There are also mini-cassette recorders that can be hidden in a pocket and carried into a meeting.

Nowadays, every office has a photocopying machine. The more security conscious the office environment, the more difficult it will be to use the machine during work hours for spying. Still, many spies find that the easiest way to make copies of a document is to copy it at the office.

Smart spies don't take just the document they want to copy to the copy machine. They hide it in a pile of regular work or some personal material, e.g., invitations to a party or a child's homework. Getting caught using the office equipment for personal work may earn a reprimand, but it will be a lot less serious than what would happen if the security officer knew about the top-secret alert list hidden under the child's drawing of a witch.

When documents cannot be copied in the location they are kept, the spy may have to remove the documents to a safe place, copy them, and then return them to their storage area. This is such a high-risk behavior that the case officer should personally approve such action, determining first if the intelligence is worth risking the permanent loss of the spy.

Despite the inherent danger in removing documents from an office, the spy can probably get away with it because most office managers get very relaxed about security. Time and again I've watched government bureaucrats make photocopies of secret documents stamped with clear warnings that no copies were to be made. They did it not because they were spies but because they wanted every person in a meeting to have a copy of the document instead of having to pass it

THE SECURITY ASPECT   161

around. In such a lax security situation, a spy might well be observed copying secret documents and still not be challenged. In his years as a spy, John Walker repeatedly made photocopies of code books and carried them home in his briefcase and never came close to getting caught. (Walker was finally caught when his ex-wife, who had known about his spying for years, turned him in to the FBI.)

Computers as Spy Tools

The use of computers has totally changed the nature of spying, mostly to the advantage of the spy. The easiest document of all to steal is a document stored in binary format in a computer, provided you have access to the computer and know how to access the information. It takes only the right kind of floppy disk and a few seconds alone to copy the desired file to the floppy disk.

Most computer security programs are designed to keep strangers out of the system, but the whole purpose of recruiting a spy is to have someone who has access to a system. The better security programs have a compartmentalized network that requires passwords to access the most sensitive information. However, a knowledgeable computer expert can often hack into such reserved areas. Better yet for the spy, those who have access to the sensitive areas of the network are often extremely careless in keeping passwords secret. They may write passwords down in a notebook; use easily discovered passwords such as their mothers' names, their addresses, or their birth dates; or get sloppy about checking to make sure that no one, not even their trusted secretaries, is looking over their shoulders when they log in.

Anyone who intends to run an espionage operation against any modern organization should be thoroughly familiar with computers and should train their recruits in the use of computers. A janitor or chauffeur everyone assumes is computer illiterate may gain access to the organization's computers at times of the day when he can browse through hard disks and network directories with minimum risk of discovery. I predict that, increasingly, the best spy of all will be the individual who has access to the organization's computer data disks.

It is not only easy to steal intelligence documents off a computer, it is also easy to smuggle the stolen documents out of the office. Computer floppy disks can be hidden in a pocket, slipped into the lining of a coat, taped to the inner thigh, or put into an envelope and mailed out of the building. The information can even be encrypted, then sent out as e-mail to the spy's home computer.

Computers in the spy's home or workplace can also be used as hiding places for stolen digital information.

The techniques of using computers as spy tools and protecting the integrity of the files are far beyond the scope of this book. Any intelligence agent intending to use a computer as part of an intelligence-collection operation should go through the following checklist:

- Don't save or store any documents you want to keep secret on the hard disk or a floppy disk with no encryption. Always work on plain text documents in RAM memory and encrypt before storing the information on disks.
- Always use a total erase program when deleting any sensitive file from a hard or floppy disk that you or your spy controls.
- Keep all sensitive information in encrypted format on floppy disks rather than the hard disk drive and have a hiding place for such disks that is located as far from the computer as is practical. Take the disks out of hiding only when working on them and return them to their hiding place immediately when you're finished.
- Most encryption systems sold on the market can be easily broken, including many that advertise they can't be broken. Many of the encryption systems bundled with word processor software are not secure. Know what makes an encryption program trustworthy.

- Even if you are sure you have the best encryption program available, double-encrypt everything, using two different systems.
- If you are sending messages by modem, always use an encryption system based on the RSA analog and a public key code. Among the best of these programs is Pretty Good Privacy, which can be found on many computer bulletin boards for free.
- Change passwords frequently. The great advantage of the RSA encryption system is that the public key passwords can be changed daily and given out in an open message.
- Be aware that it is possible to read a computer screen from a distance of up to several hundred feet with equipment that can be put together in a garage. Always take steps to ensure your computer is isolated and electromagnetic emissions are minimized.

If you don't understand what I'm talking about in any of the above points, don't put your trust in computers until you do. If you do understand what I am talking about, you will not only be able to use computers with some degree of confidence, but you will be able to quickly and easily steal computer data off the computers of most people using them.

Hiding Stolen Documents, Reports, and Computer Disks

The spy must have a secure place to hide reports, photos, film, documents, computer disks, and anything else he might steal until they can be safely delivered to the case officer. The spy should identify hiding places that include both places where he can store material for several weeks and quickly stash something in an emergency.

The more permanent storage place might be a hidden floor safe at the spy's home, a safe deposit box in a local bank, a rented storage space, a watertight box buried in the backyard, a hiding spot in an attic or a basement, or a hollowed-out spot in a wall.

The spy should identify at least one temporary hideaway in every location where he will be holding material for any period of time, even for a few minutes, in case an unexpected visitor pops in.

The temporary hiding place may be nothing more than a desk drawer with a false bottom or a picture on the wall with an envelope mounted on the back. It might be a throw rug in a corner, a piece of upholstered furniture with a small slit in the fabric, an envelope taped to the bottom side of a desk or file drawer, a plastic bag in a toilet tank, a hollowed-out book on a bookshelf, a large vase filled with artificial flowers, or even a piece of outgoing mail, stamped and addressed to a nonexistent person. Such quickie hiding places will not survive a thorough search by a professional investigator, but if a spy is singled out for that kind of treatment, his cover has already been blown.

The ability to hide material is so important that every intelligence collector should make it a habit to identify such hideaways automatically when he enters a room, even if he doesn't have anything to hide at the moment.

ESTABLISHING SECURE COMMUNICATIONS BETWEEN THE CONTROL OFFICER AND SPY

The higher the security threat level, the greater the problems associated with personal meetings between the case officer and the spy. A CIA case officer working under embassy cover in China assumes that the Chinese counterintelligence agency will have him under surveillance around the clock. The same applies for a KGB officer working out of the Soviet Embassy in Washington, D.C. So in such cases, the case officer may personally meet with a spy he controls only once every two or three years.

On the other hand, a tobacco company intelligence officer who is gathering information on an antismoking political action group doesn't have to worry too much that someone might spot him meeting with his spy inside the target group. Yet, even in this relatively secure situation, the less the people being spied on know about the case officer and his contacts with the spy, the better the security.

Fortunately, when personal contact between the two is most critical (during the recruitment phrase), the recruit will not be doing any actual spying and the risks of the operation being discovered are not as great as they will eventually be. Once the spy starts providing intelligence, he will realize that he is engaged in a dangerous activity and will be anxious to avoid detection. Therefore, he will probably concur that he should limit further contact with the case officer to occasional meetings and that he must exercise extreme caution in passing stolen information on to the case officer.

Although a case officer should handle his spies from as great a distance as is feasible, he must also establish a system for the spy to pass information to the case officer and for the spy to receive queries, instructions, and payments. This is when both the spy and his case officer are most vulnerable to identification and capture. Therefore, case officers working in dangerous circumstances, such as someone spying on the CIA for the KGB, go to great lengths to limit the direct contact between a case officer and the spy. (For example, while spying for the KGB, John Walker met with his control once every two or three years.)

Communications between control and spy in high-risk situations are often limited to some variation of publicly posted messages and the use of dead drops. Publicly posted messages are coded and placed in locations that tell either the case officer or the spy that a certain planned action should be taken. Such messages might be an advertisement in a newspaper, a poster on a bulletin board in a supermarket, a piece of graffiti on a wall, or a chalk mark on something that can be seen from the street. A dead drop is a place where documents, films, money, and other materials can be left by one party and picked up by another party with no direct contact between them.

KGB case agents operating in the United States during the Cold War preferred public mailboxes as the place to post a coded command. When Rick Ames had documents to pass to his KGB control officer, he would make a chalk mark on one of three different drop boxes situated on corners on his route to and from work. The mark would be a cross, a triangle, or some other simple design. The KGB case officer would drive by each of the letter boxes once a week or so. Whenever he saw the coded mark, he would know that Ames had something to deliver. He would then wipe the mark off the mailbox as a signal that he had seen the mark.

When Ames saw that his message had been received, he would take the packet of material to a dead drop he had already been told about. The KGB case agent handling Ames provided detailed instructions on the location of dead drops—including photos of the spot marked with a felt or a grease pen. The pictures and the text showed where to find the designated dead drop, which might be a hollow tree or a metal box hidden behind a rock in a wooded area or thick bush.

A similar dead drop arrangement is used by the case officer to deliver materials or information to the spy—e.g., special instructions for setting up a face-to-face meeting, any payment owed to the spy, and detailed directions for where the next dead drop would be. Naturally, both parties have to exercise extreme caution in approaching a dead drop to ensure that they are not under surveillance.

There are hundreds of different ways for posting disguised messages in public places. An advertisement in a newspaper's personal section might read, "John, Marsha still loves you," but mean, "I have information for you to collect at the drop." The disguised message could just as easily be something in the lost-and-found section. "One black dog who answers to Red," could really mean "You have a drop waiting at post red."

During World War II, the British government regularly passed information to agents behind German lines by coded announcements on the BBS short-wave broadcasts. Other ways of posting public messages include arranging the curtains on a window in a special way, leaving a car parked facing down the driveway instead of up, putting an item such as a child's toy in a car window while the car is parked in its usual place during the workday, or even wearing a particular item of clothing, say a hat or a topcoat not worn at other times.

Lower-Threat Security Situations

Recruiting and managing spies in low-threat situations involving private parties or commercial businesses will generally not involve the extreme communications procedures just described. Nevertheless, there is always a chance that the target of the spy operation will identify the recruit as someone who may be spying against it. If that happens, the target organization's counterespionage officers will attempt to follow the spy and identify who is receiving the stolen material. Therefore, in even a low-threat situation, the case officer must not allow anyone to identify him as someone who has regular contact with the spy if he has no good reason to be meeting with him.

Direct Visual Contact

When dealing in a security situation in which there is little chance that the intelligence target could identify the control officer as an intelligence collector, the case officer can set up occasional visual contacts under circumstances in which either the recruit or the case officer can initiate the contact when both are in the same area, if there is a need for such contact. Such approaches should appear to be a part of the regular life-style of both the recruit and the case officer. The two people might go to the same church every Sunday, eat lunch in the same restaurant once a week, regularly attend movies at the same theatre or rent videos at the same store, jog in a park at the same time each day, or use the same supermarket for weekly shopping. The case officer and the recruit can stop and talk to each other for a few moments when they meet, passing verbal information back and forth as required. They might even pick a small bar or a park bench as a meeting place.

In more security-sensitive situations, the case officer might arrange a simple series of visual signals that can be communicated if contact is desired as he and his spy pass each other or spot one another across a room or an open area. These kinds of signals are limited only by the imagination of the case officer and the setting of the assignation.

In one example, an intelligence entrepreneur who worked for a major manufacturing firm recruited a spy inside the regional Occupational Safety and Health Administration (OSHA) office. The spy's sole responsibility was to collect any information on employee complaints filed against the company so that company directors could take corrective action before an OSHA inspector showed up at the plant. The spy was an avid jogger, so the case agent began jogging on the same path as the spy a couple of times a week, but the agent ran in the opposite direction. Most of the time they would pass each other without even a nod or a smile of recognition.

Whenever the spy had something to pass on, he would wear a college sweatshirt when he jogged but would give no indication he knew the case officer when they passed on the trail. The spy would put the information in a dead drop the next day, hiding it in a plastic bag that he would toss in a trash can along the jogging path. Within minutes, the case agent would pick up the bag, retrieve the document as he jogged along, and then put an envelope with the payment in the bag and drop the bag into a second trash can along the way. The spy would pick up the payment as he passed the second trash can on his way back home.

Each of the joggers had another special sweatshirt he would wear if he had something to talk about. When the joggers saw that signal, they would pull up and stop at a drinking fountain along the way, taking time for a quick chat, but they would never exchange any material at that time.

In other situations, wearing a wristwatch on the right hand

might indicate a request for a private meeting or the need to deliver information. Placing specific items in a shopping cart, carrying a magazine under a specified arm, wearing a hat or not wearing a hat, removing and cleaning a pair of glasses, dropping something and then picking it up, or crossing one's legs while sitting on a park bench can all be arranged signals between the agent and his spy. The messages and the codes should be kept as simple as possible, limited to pretty much the following kinds of statements:

- I have material to pass to you.
- We need to meet so we can talk.
- I am being followed.
- You have a tail.
- Everything is okay.

Both the circumstances and the specific codes used should be varied, and whenever he makes a drop, the case officer should pass on new instructions to be followed until the next drop.

Making an Exchange

There are many different ways to make exchanges in low-threat security situations without allowing anyone to see the spy and the case officer exchange anything. For instance, the spy might follow the control officer into a bathroom, where each enters a stall. The spy passes a package of stolen secrets under the stall wall to the case officer. He remains seated until the case officer has left the bathroom with the package. Or two people, each carrying briefcases, board a bus at two different stops. They stand or sit near each other. When one of them gets off the bus, no one notices that they have switched suitcases.

Couriers

Some intelligence officers prefer to use couriers, usually service agents, to carry information back and forth between case officers and their recruits. Sometimes the courier is someone already inside the social circle of the recruit, but is a person whom the case officer recruited separately. Sometimes a courier may be the person who first helped entrap the recruit, such as the woman who started sleeping with him or the man who loaned him money. Sometimes a courier will be unfamiliar to and with the recruit and the material he is carrying back and forth. A case officer might even use a professional messenger service. However, all material sent by courier or messenger must first be encoded in some way.

Postal Service

Although seldom discussed in the literature of spying, the mailman delivers a good percentage of the communications between spies and their recruits. The case officer will rent a post office box, a commercial mailbox, or sometimes a small apartment or business office that will also serve as part of his false-flag cover. This allows the spy to mail whatever he has to the case officer.

It may even be possible for the spy to use the postal system at his business, government, or embassy office. All the spy has to do is drop a letter with a fake return address into a mailbox. Two days later, the case officer can pick up the information at his post office box, which is rented in a fake name and home address. For additional security, the case officer will not pick up his mail personally, but rather send a service agent who will follow standard surveillance detection and avoidance procedures before and after he has picked up the mail.

The mail can be used both ways. The recruit can also rent his own post office or commercial mailbox to which the case officer can send him mail.

It may not be necessary for the recruit to bother with private mailboxes, especially in the United States. Because of the massive amount of junk mail that is dumped into every mailbox in the country, it is easy for a case officer to send messages to a spy that are designed to look like junk mail. The piece of junk mail could be an invitation for a "free trip" to Las Vegas, an obvious sweepstakes scam, a solicitation to buy stocks or a time-share apartment, or any of the other scams used by direct-mail pitch artists. Only the recruit will recognize the piece of mail as a message from his control officer. Such a scheme may even involve secret writing: passing an iron over the message or perhaps wiping the page with a chemical solution will bring out the secret message written in the margins.

Telephone Communications

The number of daily communications during which sensitive commercial, government, and personal information is exchanged numbers in the tens of millions. Business executives discuss multibillion-dollar contracts, police officers talk about an upcoming drug bust, and thousands of men and women set up rendezvous for adultery every day and never have any fears about being tapped. At low-threat security levels, the case officer and the recruit will probably talk from time to time on the telephone. However, anyone engaging in any illegal activity takes a great risk discussing such activity over an open phone line.

Despite both the legal and technical difficulties, governments can intercept and listen in on phone lines, and they will do so if they have enough reason to focus on a single individual. If a government agency suspects that one of their employees is spying, one of the first things they will do is request telephone records and put a pen register order on the line. A pen register (used by police) will record all the numbers that any given telephone dials. Such a technical step, which is done at the telephone exchange rather than where the spy is located, does not require a court order. Therefore, once a spy comes under suspicion, law enforcement officers will quickly be able to identify every number he calls in the future and all long-distance numbers he has called in the past. At some point, the government will get enough evidence to obtain a warrant for a phone tap. Well-financed criminal organizations and large corporations can also usually find a way to tap a line, even though they will have to break the law to do it.

Anyone engaging in spying in high-risk situations should use extreme caution whenever talking on the telephone and *must assume that someone is listening to every word.*

Whether one is an intelligence officer or just an ordinary guy, the following list of telephone security rules will keep anyone out of trouble.

- Don't ever discuss any illegal activity over any telephone to which you are known to have access. If you must make a call for such a purpose, make it from a public phone to a public phone. This means that arrangements must be made in advance so that the person receiving the phone call will be monitoring the public phone when it rings.
- Whenever using a public phone or making sensitive calls from a private line, either pay with coins or with a prepaid long-distance card, which can be purchased anonymously in supermarkets, drugstores, and even the post office and cannot be traced to you. (Remember that these prepurchased telephone cards can be used to make local calls, albeit at long-distance charges.)
- Remember that the easiest way to intercept and listen in on a telephone call is to pick up an extension.
- Don't discuss sensitive information, even your credit card numbers, over any cellular, cordless, or other type of phone that transmits a radio signal.
- Don't use clever code words or trite phrases, such as calling cocaine "Coca Cola" or talking about going on a "fishing trip" when the planned activity is a recruiting session with a potential spy. If you find it necessary to talk in any kind of code, then you should be sending encrypted messages through the most sophisticated encryption systems available.
- If a phone must be used in an emergency, use a simple code to

tell the other party to go to a prearranged public or safe phone and stand by to receive a call or to call a prearranged number.

Using Computers and Modems
for Secure Communications

Just as the author cannot address all the issues of using computers in data theft, storage, and retrieval, neither can he explain in this book all of the ins and outs of using computers for secure communications between a case officer and a recruited spy. Nevertheless, if both the case officer and the recruit have access to a modern computer, a modem, and a telephone line, then the case officer will want to take advantage of the World Wide Web and e-mail.

Because all modem signals travel through commercial telephone lines, they present all the same security problems that the telephone presents. Phone lines can easily be tapped by law enforcement officers or anyone who has access to the interior of the building or the phone connection box. People who tap phones will have computers and modems, too. Send an open message by modem and they will read it before the addressee sees it.

Even so, computers and modems can make communications much more secure than a simple phone call, provided the operators understand the technology and the systems—as well as their limitations.

E-Mail

The first advantage of computer communication is e-mail. Anyone with an Internet connection or a connection to such commercial information services as CompuServe, America Online, or Prodigy can send anyone a message, any place in the world, by connecting with a local number. Pen registers and phone records will show only the number of the Internet server or the information service.

No e-mail message is secure unless it is encrypted with a sophisticated encryption program. It can be intercepted while it is in the office network, on the Internet, stored in the hard drives of the computer information service, and in transmission. E-mail messages are also on the hard disks of every computer they pass through, often for long periods, even after they have supposedly been erased. Much of the Irangate scandal that so badly damaged the Reagan administration's public image resulted because people like Lt. Col. Oliver North didn't realize how public e-mail can be and how complicated it is to erase e-mail so that it can never be recovered at any point along the line of transmission. No one should ever write anything in an open e-mail message that he wouldn't write down on a piece of paper and toss out the window for anyone to read.

Despite the many security risks, e-mail does provide a quick and easy way to post public messages, i.e., messages that appear to be innocent but are in fact coded instructions. Internet newsgroups, discussion groups on the commercial services, and thousands of private computer bulletin boards provide places where anyone can post a message as part of an ongoing public discussion. Literally thousands of different subjects are continually debated in such open forums with little or no limitation on who can post a message or what can be said. Insults are traded back and forth, and a lot of illogical nonsense floats through the discussions.

To set up a system of public messages, both parties have to do the following three things: 1) know the e-mail address or cover name each will be using, 2) agree on the public discussion group they will use and the coded wording to be used, and 3) know the time frame for checking messages. For example, the case officer checks the news group alt.talk.guns on a daily basis, watching for a message posted by were.dog@supercom.com. When he finds such a message and it includes the word *colt*, he knows that there is a package waiting for him at the drop site.

This is a much better means of posting public messages than buying an ad in a newspaper and running a coded message or making marks on mailboxes.

Encrypted E-Mail

Some computer encryption programs make it possible to send e-mail messages in an encrypted format that may be so secure that even the National Security Agency's computers won't be able to break the encryption. Again, any case officer who doesn't know a lot about encryption should not attempt to use computer encryption in a high-risk security situation. But those who do understand this esoteric subject can send e-mail to anyone in the world with a reasonable expectation that the message will be read only by the recipient.

Encrypted e-mail messages can be sent through the Internet, commercial computer information services, private bulletin boards, or direct computer-to-computer phone connections.

However, there is one serious problem with an encrypted message: the mere fact that it is encrypted will be seen as evidence that both parties are engaged in some kind of illegal, immoral, or disloyal behavior. If a government agency suspects that an employee is spying and it taps a line and discovers that he is sending encrypted messages to someone, the bureaucrats will take that as proof of spying.

The way to avoid this problem is to take the same precautions that you do to talk on the telephone. Both parties use public phones, and if the calls are long-distance, they pay with either coins or, better, the prepaid telephone cards. Besides encryption, another advantage of computer communication is that both parties don't have to be on the line at the same time to communicate.

A scenario such as the following might work. Earl Harden, a real estate speculator, recruits Dennis Powers, an engineer working for the City Highway Commission, to copy files out of the commission's computer that describe future city highway construction routes. On the first Saturday of each month, Harden checks into a hotel under the name of Craig Beasily. He attaches the modem of his desktop computer to his room telephone and sets the computer software so that it will answer the phone when it rings. (Harden doesn't have to wait in the hotel room for the call.)

Sometime during the day, Dennis Powers takes his notebook computer to the city airport where there is a courtesy office for business travelers. He connects his modem to the phone at a courtesy desk and, using his prepaid calling card, calls the hotel and asks to be connected to Craig Beasily's room. When the computer in the hotel room answers, Dennis punches the right commands, and his computer downloads the latest stolen data in encrypted format to Harden's computer. He then downloads a file from Harden's computer, which passes on instructions for future contacts. Later in the day, Harden picks up his computer and pays his hotel bill in cash.

REDUCING PERSONAL CONTACTS

Obviously, you should avoid personal contact as much as possible. But even in high-risk situations, both the control officer and the recruit will occasionally have to meet face-to-face. Sometimes, the spy may request such a meeting to ask for more money or explain why he can't produce everything the case officer expects of him. More often, it will be the case officer who will request the meeting, perhaps to provide some additional training and guidance, administer a polygraph test, or do an in-depth interview to evaluate the honesty of the spy's reporting.

The case officer must remain in control when it comes to arranging meetings, even when it is the spy who is requesting the personal contact. The case officer must decide where and when to meet and how the recruit will travel to the meeting place. He should pick meeting places where he is totally familiar with the layout and the ordinary traffic through the area.

Government intelligence case officers working in high-risk situations will prefer, if at all possible, to hold meetings with recruited spies in a third country, preferably one in which the local government is more friendly toward the government who is running the spy. Remember that the Mossad seldom puts its case agents in a hostile Arab country. It recruits Arabs as spies while they are traveling in Western countries and holds all meetings with such spies in friendly Western countries. In the case of Rick Ames, the KGB control officer would meet with him in Colombia while Rick and his wife were visiting her mother.

Even those who are engaged in private intelligence collection are well advised to meet with the spies they control in another state, another region of the country, or even another country. The farther they are from home territory, the less likely it is that the relationship will be accidentally exposed.

If the spy cannot travel to a distant place or a foreign country, then the case officer will have to identify a secure place where the meeting can be held closer to home. In low-threat situations, the case officer may decide to meet in some public place, say a park or restaurant. However, if the session will include training or last a long time, the case officer will want to arrange for a safe house.

Safe Houses

A safe house is any private place controlled by the case officer or his agents, which has not been identified by any counterespionage or security agency. It may be a rental house on a large piece of property or an apartment, but it works better if the apartment is not in a building that has a doorman or a security system. Hotel rooms can also be used as a safe house. When the room is rented just before a meeting is scheduled, the case officer can be reasonably certain that the room is secure, especially if he or one of his agents picks up the spy at another spot and takes him to the hotel.

It is always best if the recruit doesn't know prior to the meeting where the safe house is. He should be picked up at another site and taken to the safe house. If the case officer intends to continue to use the safe house, the spy should be blindfolded or perhaps travel in the back of a truck or van so he can't see the route of travel.

Whenever the case officer meets one of his spies, the case

officer must always arrive at the selected site before the recruit. Someone working for the case officer should keep the recruit under surveillance from the time he departs for the meeting until after he has returned to his home or place of business. If the case officer or his agents spot anyone surveilling the recruit, the meeting site, or the case officer, the meeting must be aborted and the case officer should leave the area immediately.

If the meeting includes a training session or a trip to a foreign country, the spy must have a good cover story to explain his absence to his employer and family. Although it may never be used, the cover story should include *innocent* explanations for the spy's actions at every point during the trip, from his home or office to the location of the meeting.

The best cover stories are those that include several different layers of deception. In one example, a Colombian drug ring had recruited an informant inside the Coast Guard office responsible for drug interdiction on the high seas. The drug cartel case officer wanted three days with the informant, a young flight lieutenant, to train him in the use of a sophisticated computer communication system the spy would be using to send his reports to Colombia via the Internet. The drug lords, through a company they controlled in Mexico, set up a tourist promotional contest that offered a week's vacation in Cancun, Mexico.

The lieutenant entered and won the rigged contest and took the trip. After he checked into a hotel in Cancun, he met a pretty Argentinean woman at the hotel bar in what would have appeared to any surveillance to be a casual pickup. The Argentine was an expensive international prostitute who had been hired by the drug cartel but who had no idea she was working for drug traffickers. She carried a sealed envelope of instructions that she gave to the Coast Guard officer as soon as they were alone in a hotel room.

After spending the night with the woman, the lieutenant called his office back home and told his secretary that he was taking a car excursion to visit the ruins in the Yucatán

Peninsula for the day. He then rented a car and asked for a map of the Yucatán before driving away with the Latin American woman by his side.

Following the instructions, they drove to a Mexican town on the river across from Belize. The two checked into the best hotel in town. The lieutenant then deliberately disabled the rental car and left it in a local repair shop to be fixed. A van picked him up as he walked back to the hotel and took him to a ranch several miles outside of town and on the Belize side of the river where the lieutenant spent two days in training. The Argentinean woman stayed in the hotel room in town, ordering room service for two and keeping the "Do Not Disturb" sign hung on the door. (The cartel supplied another woman, one who spoke no English, for the lieutenant's pleasure during his two nights at the ranch.)

When the lieutenant finally returned to his hotel in Cancun, he called his secretary and described an unfortunate story of his car breaking down and his spending uncomfortable nights in a small Mexican town. No one ever checked his story, but if someone had, that person would have discovered the lieutenant's secret sexual escapade, but no evidence that he had ever entered Belize from Mexico.

Chapter Fifteen

Case Studies

The following studies demonstrate the different techniques and plots that can be used to recruit a spy. Readers should ask themselves how they would have created the scenario, what stage decorations they would have used, how they would have approached the target for recruitment, and how they would have led the target into treason.

CATCHING QADDAFI'S FLUNKY

In 1980, Khalid Al-Daraji, a Libyan munitions expert, was working on the Libyan air defense program. His duties sometimes required stays of several weeks in Rome as part of the Libyan effort to buy high-tech air defense weapons from European firms willing to trade technology for petro-dollars. Khalid always left his wife and family in Libya when making such trips. The CIA identified Khalid as a possible recruit who might tell it something about Libyan air defenses. CIA intelligence officers working undercover in the U.S. Embassy in Rome designed and implemented a plan to entrap Khalid the next time he showed up in Rome.

As was his custom, on his next trip to Rome Khalid stayed

in a small hotel apartment and took the bus each day to his office in the Libyan Embassy. As he was waiting one morning at the bus stop, a young Italian woman walked up and stood waiting beside him. She smiled at him, but neither spoke. A few minutes later, a large sedan pulled up to the curb, driven by a middle-aged man dressed in a business suit; the woman got into the car, and off they drove.

For the next three days, Khalid found the woman waiting for her ride when he arrived at the bus stop. She was always the only other person standing there. While she always smiled at him, and a couple of times said good morning, the shy Khalid never tried to start a conversation. Each day the man in the car came by and picked her up.

On the fifth day, the car didn't show up at the usual time. The woman didn't look worried about the failure of her ride to appear, and about five minutes later she boarded a bus that always passed the stop just a few minutes before Khalid's bus came by.

Less than 30 seconds after the bus had pulled away, the man in the car pulled up to the stop. He rolled his window down and asked Khalid if he had seen the woman he usually picked up. Khalid answered that the woman had just taken a bus. The man thanked Khalid, and then, in what appeared to be an afterthought, asked Khalid where he was going. When Khalid told him, the man said he was going that way and offered Khalid a ride into the city center, which he accepted.

The driver of the car, who spoke English with a British public school accent, introduced himself as Matthew Clark. He explained that the woman, Eva, and he worked in the same building. He gave her a ride whenever it was convenient.

For the next several days, when Clark stopped to pick up Eva, he also offered Khalid a ride. As they rode along, Matthew directed the conversation mostly at Khalid, asking him about North Africa and Libyan culture. Matthew also talked a little about himself and his business, which was putting together international trade deals for a German trade consortium. By the third day he was asking Khalid questions about the Libyan economy and the possibilities for trade opportunities in Libya.

When the conversation drifted into a discussion of restaurants on the fourth day, Matthew asked Khalid's recommendation for a good North African restaurant. When Khalid replied that he almost never ate in restaurants, Matthew insisted that Khalid go to dinner with him that evening. Khalid accepted the invitation but suggested he would prefer to try a good French restaurant. Matthew took the suggestion as evidence that while Khalid was enjoying his new friendship, he did not want to risk running into anyone from the Libyan Embassy while in the company of a European. Matthew then asked Eva to join them as he planned on taking Martha. (It was the first time that Matthew had mentioned he had a woman in his life.) At dinner, Matthew introduced Martha as a business associate, although they acted more like lovers. Khalid found Eva a very friendly dinner partner, who was obviously interested in him as a man.

Thus began a four-way friendship that quickly became an important part of Khalid's Roman experience, but one he never mentioned to his Libyan colleagues at the embassy. Khalid especially wanted to keep his romance with Eva, which had blossomed during the first dinner engagement, a secret from his Libyan compatriots. That very night, Eva had invited Khalid to her own apartment, just down the block from Khalid's apartment, and made love to him. After that, Khalid and Eva frequently went out to dinner with Matthew and Martha, with Matthew always picking up the check.

Increasingly, Matthew focused the conversation when they were together on possible trade opportunities for his firm in Libya. When Khalid talked enthusiastically about several different possibilities for trade, Matthew asked if Khalid could put some of his thoughts down on paper, promising to pay Khalid if the report proved useful in discovering possible Libyan trade opportunities.

Khalid prepared such a report, which contained nothing of a sensitive nature. Matthew praised the information and a day later passed Khalid an envelope stuffed with Italian bank notes, which he claimed was payment from his partners. Khalid used most of the money to buy an expensive present for Eva, who was now sleeping at his apartment almost every night. Khalid, whose circumcised wife back in Iran found sex a painful experience that she endured as seldom as possible, was getting the best sex of his life and doing a lot of pillow-talk bragging about the important work he was doing for his country.

On two more occasions, Matthew asked Khalid to write reports on economic and political developments in Libya, paying him well for each effort. The next time that Matthew asked for a report, he requested that Khalid jot down specific comments on Qaddafi's political future and the possibility of his overthrow.

Khalid's first attempt quoted the official Libyan line, saying only the nicest things possible about Qaddafi. Matthew rejected that attempt and refused to pay for it, insisting that Khalid write the truth as he knew it, not Libyan propaganda. At the same time, Eva was suggesting that she and Khalid fly to a Mediterranean resort for a weekend getaway, an expense that Khalid had no way to pay for unless he could collect another payment from Matthew.

After a couple of days, Khalid gave Matthew a report on Qaddafi that criticized the dictator and described a number of atrocities he knew Qaddafi had committed. Even so, the report predicted that Qaddafi had a permanent hold on power and that he would probably rule until the day he died of old age. Khalid begged Matthew not to divulge to anyone who had prepared the report, and Matthew promised that Khalid had nothing to worry about. Matthew paid Khalid enough to splurge in a big way on his weekend with Eva.

The next time Matthew asked Khalid for more information, he asked for information on the Libyan air defense system, explaining that his trade consortium hoped to outbid the current suppliers for the Libyan government purchases. Matthew assured Khalid that he would be serving Libya's best interests because Matthew's consortium would be able to supply better, more modern equipment at a bargain price. However, in order to make an offer that would impress Khalid's bosses in the Libyan government, Matthew needed details on what kind of equipment the Libyans had already purchased, who had supplied the equipment, how much they had paid for the equipment, and how the equipment was positioned to defend Tripoli and Benghazi.

Matthew promised Khalid that if his information made a deal possible, he would make Khalid a secret partner and Khalid might well make a hundred thousand British pounds or more. Matthew suggested that in anticipation of such wealth, Khalid ought to open a secret Swiss bank account and gave a bit of advice on how Khalid could do that.

Both Eva and Martha listened as Matthew made his proposal. As soon as she and Khalid were alone, Eva began talking excitedly about the expected money, and that night, Khalid experienced the best sex ever. In the morning, Eva suggested that if Khalid earned the expected money, he might set her up in an apartment in Tripoli as a permanent part of his life.

Khalid had to rewrite the report on Libyan air defenses several times, each time adding more detail at Matthew's insistence. By the time the report met Matthew's demands, Khalid must have realized that he was selling his nation's closely guarded secrets. He no doubt continued to tell himself, however, that he was selling those secrets to people who would never use them against Libya.

In fact, the information provided by Khalid played a key role in the planning for the U.S. air attack on Tripoli on April 14, 1986.

Matthew Clark was a CIA case officer working under a false flag. He was backed up by a team of a dozen agents.

Martha was a CIA expert on air defenses assigned to the case to provide technical advice to the CIA case officer. Eva was a very expensive Italian prostitute who had no more idea of the true identity of Matthew than Khalid did. The original plan was that Khalid would take the hint at the bus stop and start flirting with Eva, which in turn would lead to a date and then sex, after which she would introduce him to Matthew. When the shy Khalid didn't take the bait, Matthew changed the plan and made the approach by offering Khalid a ride. From there, things went according to plan.

WHO'S THE SPY?

Lester Stapler got caught up in what is perhaps the most convoluted spy recruitment involving a false flag ever put in place. Stapler had been employed as a civilian intelligence analyst for the Defense Intelligence Agency (DIA) for seven years. Then he left the agency and started his own private international consulting firm.

Working under contract with a U.S. airline company, Stapler went to Mexico City on an extended business trip. While there, he was approached by George Brennan and Kenneth Brauer, who identified themselves as CIA intelligence officers attached to the U.S. Embassy in Mexico City. They said they knew about his previous employment with the DIA and asked him for assistance in setting up a scam to penetrate the KGB operation in Mexico, telling him he would be serving his country while making some good money. They explained they wanted Stapler to pretend to be a financially strapped U.S. businessman who wanted to cash in on things he knew about the DIA by selling information to the local KGB resident.

The two CIA agents assured Stapler that he would be working as a contract employee of the CIA while performing the service. He was given a civil service application form to fill out, W-2 forms, and applications for insurance and death benefits, as well as the standard security clearance update forms.

Stressing that it was critically important that Stapler convince the Soviet resident that he had information worth selling, George and Ken told Stapler to give the Soviet agent a lot of detail about his work at the DIA. When Stapler expressed some hesitation in doing that, fearing he might let slip some secrets, the three men spent several days in a hotel room going over what Stapler could tell the Soviet agent about his previous employment and what he shouldn't mention.

During those long sessions, the two CIA men had Stapler describe in detail what he did during his seven-year career at the DIA. They drafted several dozen different messages to the CIA headquarters asking for specific clearance for what things Stapler could release and what things he should not mention.

The two CIA men also gave Stapler a direct phone number at the embassy where he could contact them. Stapler called the number several times. The phone was always answered by a female secretary speaking American-style English with a slight Mexican accent and telling the caller he had reached the U.S. Embassy.

During the long sessions in hotel rooms, the two intelligence officers frequently talked on the telephone with someone at the embassy while Stapler listened to their side of the conversation. They also showed Stapler the answers to the messages they had sent to Washington.

The three men eventually developed a playbook of specific things that Stapler could tell the Soviet case agent once contact had been made. The final script ended up being so bland that Stapler expressed some concern that it wouldn't be enough to satisfy the Soviet officer. Nevertheless, the two CIA men insisted that once contact had been made, Stapler would not give the Soviet agent anything he wasn't authorized by Washington to give.

When the two CIA agents were satisfied that Stapler was ready, they directed him to make contact with the Soviet agent, pretending to be a walk-in. Stapler walked into the Soviet Embassy in Mexico and gave the story about wanting to sell secrets. He was soon talking to an agent who called himself Boris. Stapler followed the script approved by the CIA headquarters and reported back to Brennan and Brauer after the meeting. The two CIA agents were ecstatic, telling Stapler that he had met with Boris Komplektov, one of the top KGB case officers in Mexico.

Stapler met several more times with Boris, who insisted with increasing agitation that Stapler provide more sensitive information as proof of his sincerity. Boris' demands for more detailed information resulted in more long discussions with the two CIA men over what Stapler might tell the Soviet agent. The two CIA men drafted more cables and a day later showed Stapler the replies, which denied permission to give any more sensitive information to the Soviet intelligence officer than what Langley had already approved.

Stapler met once more with Boris, who abruptly terminated the conversation and told Stapler that the information he was trying to peddle was worthless. When Stapler reported back to George and Kenneth, they thanked Stapler for his cooperation, agreeing with Stapler that the ploy hadn't worked because of the CIA's unwillingness to throw more truth into the equation.

The two CIA men did insist that all had not been lost: they had at least learned a few things about how the KGB handled a walk-in. They stressed the importance of keeping the whole thing secret and showed Stapler a request they were submitting for a substantial bonus for Stapler's services. They promised Stapler that the U.S. Treasury Department would issue a check, which would be mailed to his U.S. bank account. Stapler's next bank statement showed the money had been deposited as promised.

This might have ended the whole affair, except that several weeks later when he was back home in the States, Stapler read a news article reporting that the U.S. Embassy in Mexico City had an office of the FBI that monitored Americans seen entering the Soviet Embassy, which was suspected of being a favorite spot for would-be spies to make contact with Soviet intelligence officers.

Based on his own experience working in the U.S. intelligence community, Stapler was only too aware of how interagency competition sometimes kept the right hand from learning what the left was doing. Increasingly concerned that the FBI might have seen him talking to the Soviet agent and that the CIA may not have bothered to tell the FBI about its little attempt to entrap a KGB officer, Stapler tried to contact George Brennan and Kenneth Brauer, using the embassy number they had given him.

A recording in Spanish told him that number was no longer in service. Stapler found the listed number for the U.S. Embassy, called it, and was told no one by those names was now or ever had worked in the embassy. Stapler then decided to go to the FBI, describe what had happened, and make sure he wasn't on some FBI list of potential spies.

He immediately found himself accused of spying, based on his interview with the FBI in which he admitted having met with Boris in Mexico City. The FBI did have a record of his visits with Boris, and the FBI agents assumed that Stapler, having realized that the FBI must have been watching, was trying to divert suspicion by claiming he was working for the CIA. The FBI insisted that they had checked with the CIA, which denied having any employees named George Brennan and Kenneth Brauer.

It took several years for the case to work through the court system. The CIA insisted in response to court summonses that they had no employees by the name of George Brennan and Kenneth Brauer, nor did they have any record that Lester Stapler had every performed any service for the CIA while in Mexico City. A belated check with Stapler's bank uncovered that the payment he had received had been a cashier's check drawn on a Mexican bank and the source could not be traced.

While the FBI remains convinced that Stapler was a walk-in whom the KGB rejected, others in the intelligence game have concluded that Stapler was the victim of a very clever false-flag setup.

The men Stapler knew as George Brennan and Kenneth Brauer may have been Soviet intelligence case officers, or they could have been case officers working for any of a dozen other intelligence services. They could have even been spying for one of the several different antigovernment groups that are constantly criticizing U.S. intelligence agencies.

Whoever they were, they had no doubt targeted Stapler with the intent of learning everything he might tell them about his work with the DIA. When they discovered he was going to Mexico City on a business trip, they saw it as the perfect opportunity. Using false ID, they had set up an office where they could produce what looked to Stapler like official embassy telegrams. The supposed embassy number they gave Stapler was a front manned by some woman who had probably never been near the real U.S. Embassy. The long sessions in which Stapler thought he and the two CIA handlers were determining what he could and couldn't tell a Soviet intelligence agent about his previous work were really opportunities for the two fake CIA case officers to learn just about everything about DIA analysts that they could.

WHY RECRUIT A HOTEL MAID?

Sometimes access agents can be as important as a primary agent might be in other circumstances. Charlene Brevis was the night housekeeper for a commercial hotel in a major midwestern city. Charlene was also a single mother who had three teenaged children. When her only son died as an innocent victim in a drug shoot-out, Charlene joined a parents' organization that was campaigning for stricter enforcement of drug laws.

About six months later, a man named Ray Kelleher started attending the meetings and introduced himself to Charlene. After a couple more meetings, Ray focused the kind of attention on Charlene that suggested a possible romance. Ray didn't talk much about himself but did listen sympathetically as Charlene talked about her dead son and her hopes for college educations for her two daughters.

The night they became lovers, Ray told Charlene that he was an undercover agent for the state police narcotics squad but asked her to keep that information confidential. As their romance blossomed, Ray often talked about the frustrations of his job and how difficult it was to get evidence on kingpin drug dealers. He confided that he and his colleagues had learned that several big drug dealers often checked into the hotel where Charlene worked. Ray was certain that the dealers were discussing major deals in their hotel rooms. Ray suggested that if there was only some way to sneak into the rooms where the drug dealers stayed, he might be able to find evidence or plant a microphone to gather such evidence. Unfortunately, without doing that, he couldn't even gather enough evidence to ask for a legal search or phone tap warrant.

Because of Charlene's anger about drug dealers, Ray didn't have too much trouble convincing her during the next several weeks that she could do a real service for the war on drugs if she would provide Ray with pass keys, which would allow him access to any room in the hotel that he suspected was being used by drug dealers.

Although Ray warned Charlene that she must keep her help a secret, he also told her he had arranged with his superiors to list Charlene as a confidential informant and she would be well paid for her assistance. Charlene began loaning Ray a set of pass keys almost every night, and she also started putting substantial amounts of money into a special bank account that would eventually help ensure her two daughters got a chance to go to college.

Several weeks later, Ray showed Charlene a newspaper story reporting the arrest of a major group of Colombian drug traffickers engaged in a money-laundering scheme. Ray claimed the arrest was the direct result of information he had collected from the hotel room where one of the conspirators had stayed. After that, Ray continued to point out occasional news stories of big drug busts, which he claimed had resulted from Charlene's cooperation.

Ray Kelleher's real name was Steven Kissman, and he was not a police officer. In fact, he had a police record as a confidence man. The only thing he knew about the drug cases he claimed to have helped solve was what he read in the papers. He and several other colleagues had found a new profession in industrial and commercial intelligence. What he really was after was access to the notebook computers so many business executives carry with them whenever they travel.

Ray would use the pass keys Charlene provided to enter the hotel rooms of business travelers while they were dining, taking in the city's entertainment, or even sleeping in their hotel rooms in the early morning hours. Ray carried his own notebook computer along on his forays, which he would use to download the contents of any notebook computer he located in a guest's bedroom. On those occasions when the businessman was sleeping in his bed, Ray would take the computer out of the room to an empty room where he would cruise through the files and download key data before returning the computer to the owner's room. Ray and his colleagues would then go over the data, identifying information that could be sold to foreign competitors of the U.S. business corporations.

Eventually, Ray's luck ran out: one of his victims woke up while he had her computer in another room. Finding that she couldn't go back to sleep, the woman decided to do some work and discovered that her computer was missing. The city police investigated the theft, and Charlene's company spent significant amounts of money on private detectives but were unable to recover the computer or discover who had taken it.

Charlene, however, immediately figured out who must have stolen the computer. When she confronted Ray, he admitted that he had taken it but pointed out that if he were caught, she would go down with him. The sizable bank account Charlene had accumulated would convince any jury that she was part of the gang.

Charlene still works for Ray, but no longer shares her bed with the lover-turned blackmailer. He still pays her for her services, but not nearly as much as when she thought she was working with the narcs. She is not the only hotel employee in the city working for Ray and his partners. In each case, the team used a different scheme in recruiting someone who could give them access to the rooms of businessmen traveling with notebook computers filled with data.

CATCH A MAN WHEN HE'S DOWN

Wilber H. Schott worked as an engineer for Eden Electronics Production, a large government weapons contractor. Schott, whose work involved the design of such high-tech weapons-guidance systems as those demonstrated during the Gulf War, had a top-secret U.S. government security clearance. After 20 years on the job, Schott failed to get the promotion he had expected, mainly because his personal life was falling apart and impacting his work performance.

In his early 50s, Schott soon found himself newly divorced with financial troubles that forced him to file personal bankruptcy. Reduced to living in a rented efficiency apartment while he worked at a job with little hope of promotion, his only recreation was an occasional game of tennis played on the apartment complex's tennis court. It was there he met Jerzy Kwasniewski, a Polish businessman. Kwasniewski played at about the same level as Schott, although Schott regularly won about two out of three games.

After a couple of weeks, Schott invited Kwasniewski up to his apartment after a game for a couple of beers. From there, their relationship developed into a friendship with lots of technical talk about developments in electronics and the efforts of Poland to find potential customers for some of the new products Polish industry was manufacturing. When Kwasniewski asked Schott to write down a list of possible U.S. customers to whom Kwasniewski might try to sell, Wilber agreed to do so.

A couple of weeks later, Kwasniewski knocked on Schott's door and excitedly announced that the information Schott provided had resulted in a substantial sale. Kwasniewski then insisted on paying Schott a finder's fee for the information that had made the sale possible.

Schott had been trained as part of his employment to recognize hostile intelligence activity. He chose to ignore the obvious signals and happily accepted the cash payment, which he spent on back rent and a couple of much-needed new suits. Over the next several months, Kwasniewski paid Schott fees for similar kinds of inconsequential information and reports on six different occasions. Each time the fees increased in size. Initially, Schott used the money to pay for necessities, but eventually he had a bit left over to pay for luxuries, including a return to the dating game.

Shortly after Schott began seriously dating a woman with two young children, Kwasniewski asked to see some unclassified but sensitive material on radar fire control for tanks to which Schott had access. Claiming he wanted the information so he could advise his home office on possible areas in which it should direct research projects, Kwasniewski promised a substantial payment as a consulting fee for good information.

Schott thought it over for a few days, then copied the material from company files and passed the information on to Kwasniewski. The payment he earned was enough to allow Schott to buy a small engagement ring and propose marriage to the new woman in his life.

From that point, it was an easy task for Kwasniewski to ask for confidential and eventually secret information. Schott knew what he was doing but kept telling himself that as soon as he got set financially, he would cut the relation with Kwasniewski, who was already talking about an expected transfer back to his home office in Poland, a transfer that Schott assumed would end the relationship.

When Kwasniewski did get the promised transfer, he proposed that he give Schott and his new wife a belated honeymoon trip to Innsbruck, Austria, in appreciation for the great help that Schott had given him during his stay in the United States. In Innsbruck, Kwasniewski spent three days showing Schott and his wife the tourist sites.

On the fourth day, Kwasniewski invited Schott to a final tennis game at a local club while Schott's wife went shopping. While they were playing on a private court, a man whom Kwasniewski introduced as the person who would be replacing him as Schott's contact appeared. When Schott discovered that Kwasniewski expected that he would continue to turn over classified information on weapons systems to the new control, Schott angrily insisted that he had no intention of doing so.

At that point, the new control officer, who had none of Kwasniewski's subtlety, pulled out of his pocket an envelope and spread out a collection of pictures showing Schott's new stepchildren. The first pictures had been taken as the children walked away from the home of a neighbor where they were staying while their mother and new stepfather enjoyed the sights of Austria. The series of pictures followed the teenaged children to school and to some extracurricular activities after school.

The new control officer then grimly announced that not only was Schott going to continue providing information, but that he was going to spend the last two days of his Innsbruck vacation undergoing some intensive training to make him a more useful spy. The new control officer suggested that Schott suddenly suffer a flu attack. Kwasniewski would then take the wife on some tours while Schott stayed in the hotel room and "nursed his flu" while the training took place.

At the end of the training session, the new control officer rewarded Schott with a $7,000 payment for his good behavior just before the Schotts boarded the plane to return home. He also provided Schott with detailed requests for specific information he wanted, as well as instructions for how to pass such information on through. Schott continued to pass information to the Polish intelligence service for several years. He was paid well for the information he provided, but he was spying more out of fear than greed.

Schott fit all the classic profile characteristics of a highly recruitable spy: marital problems that ended in divorce, financial problems, job dissatisfaction, an open friendship with a Soviet bloc national—all followed by sudden, unexplained wealth and frequent foreign travel. (He, his wife, and sometimes the two teenagers made several more trips to Innsbruck over the next few years.) But no U.S. spy-catcher unearthed him. A Polish defector eventually turned Schott in.

KNOCK HIM DOWN AND PICK HIM UP

After 15 years with the DEA, Wayne Kramer considered himself to be a hard-charging special agent on the promotion fast track. Assigned to a special money-laundering task force in South Florida, Wayne was tasked with dealing with a number of state law enforcement officials as well as several high-ranking executives in the banking community who were cooperating with law enforcement to spot money-laundering operations.

In his spare time, Wayne and his wife were also active in a church group engaged in drug-education activities aimed at high school students. While working with the church group, Wayne met Robert Shanklin, who had recently moved to Florida after retiring from a job as a deputy prosecuting attorney in a northern state. Despite the differences in their ages, the two men developed a mutual friendship because of Shanklin's strong advocacy of federal drug-enforcement programs.

During one of their conversations, Wayne confided in the older Shanklin that he was expecting to be promoted to the position of task force director when the current director got his expected promotion to the DEA's Washington headquarters.

A month before the expected promotion was to be announced, a Florida State Police agency discovered evidence while investigating one of their cases that implicated Wayne Kramer in a money-laundering scheme. Kramer angrily proclaimed his innocence, but the investigation into the charges took several months, during which time Kramer was placed on administrative leave. Another officer got the promotion that Kramer thought would be his.

The federal investigation failed to find enough evidence to convict Kramer, and he was eventually returned to full duty with no loss of pay. Kramer and his wife, however, had to take out a second mortgage on their home to pay for the legal services Kramer employed to help prove his innocence.

As is so often the case in such situations, upon his return to duty, Kramer found that many of his colleagues still thought he was guilty. Although he still had a job on the task force, Kramer was working for a supervisor he considered incompetent. Worse, he knew he would never get another promotion. The only reason he stuck it out was because he would be eligible for early retirement in seven years.

Through the hard times, the one friend who stuck with Kramer was Robert Shanklin. Shanklin not only insisted that he believed Kramer to be innocent, he loaned Kramer money for legal fees and helped him find the attorney who eventually got the charges dropped.

Shortly after Kramer returned to duty, Shanklin suggested that the person who had tried to frame Wayne was probably a jealous colleague who had sold out to the drug lords. Shanklin proposed that he (Shanklin) begin his own private investigation, using his considerable experience as a prosecutor to find out what happened.

At Shanklin's suggestion, the two men started examining every one of Kramer's colleagues who had worked on the task force prior to the discovery of the evidence that seemed to implicate Kramer in a drug deal. Shanklin assured Kramer that if they kept digging into each person's caseload, they would eventually discover something that didn't match up—perhaps a sure case that suddenly fell apart, an investigation that turned sour, or even some evidence of unexplained wealth by a colleague.

Kramer knew that he was sharing with Shanklin a great deal of information on DEA personnel, ongoing investigations, and even the identity of confidential informants, but Kramer was so determined to discover who had framed him that he felt justified in accepting Shanklin's help and providing him all information needed for the investigation.

After several months of such activity, Shanklin told Kramer that he was increasingly convinced that the colleague who had gotten the promotion Kramer had lost was a dirty cop who had deliberately framed Kramer so he could cover his own tracks as well as get the promotion. Shanklin suggested that the dirty cop was now using his position as the director of the task force to protect the crooks who paid him off while taking the competition out of circulation.

Kramer did not immediately go to his superiors with Shanklin's evidence; instead Shanklin and he started planning how they would catch the new task force director with his hand in the till. Looking for a scheme that would trap the suspected dirty cop, Kramer shared even more confidential information on active cases, hoping to spot a case where the dirty colleague had tipped off one of the drug dealers of a pending arrest.

Suddenly, in a single week, several of the task force's major cases went sour. Three prime witnesses, including a high-ranking bank officer, were gunned down in gang-style killings, five suspects targeted for arrest suddenly left the country, and when the task force served a search warrant that was supposed to catch major evidence based on wiretap information, they found nothing.

Every agent on the task force suddenly found himself answering tough questions as the supervisors tried to identify the source of a major information leak. Wayne, assuming that somehow his "crooked" supervisor had discovered the plan that Shanklin and he were about to put into play, tried to contact Shanklin to discuss what they could do next. Shanklin didn't answer his phone, and when Kramer checked out the condo where he lived, no one answered the door.

Badly shaken, Wayne found himself once again a primary suspect in the investigation. When Wayne failed a lie-detector test question about whether he had ever revealed confidential information to an unauthorized source, he tried to explain to one of the DEA's internal affairs investigators exactly what Shanklin and he had been doing. A subsequent investigation discovered that there was no such person as Robert Shanklin and certainly no evidence that the new task force supervisor had been dealing with criminals.

The investigators eventually concluded that Robert Shanklin was working with a major Colombian drug trafficking group, which had deliberately set out to infiltrate the DEA money-laundering task force. Shanklin, or someone with whom he was working had probably planted the evidence that cost Wayne Kramer his promotion—probably because at that time Kramer and those under his supervision were all found to be incorruptible. Then Shanklin—who already had Kramer convinced of his false identity—moved in, pretending to be the friend in need.

Shanklin's skill in pretending to be a retired prosecutor suggests that he may well have worked as a prosecutor at some time under another identity. He had likely been recruited by the drug cartel at that point and had continued to work for them after retirement.

Shanklin didn't share the information he tricked out of Kramer with everyone, only with a select group of traffickers and money launderers who worked for one segment of the Cali Cartel. (The task force still got a number of convictions.) In effect, the cartel got a double bonus: they escaped prosecution and put the competition out of business and in the can.

Kramer's supervisor decided that rather than go public with what Kramer had done and prosecute him for leaking confidential information, the task force would take the credit for the drug dealers and money launderers they did catch and not tell anyone about the bigger fish that got away because a clever drug cartel intelligence agent first knocked Kramer down and then picked him up.

Kramer was even permitted to stay on with the agency, although he was transferred to a small office along the California/Mexico border. Six months after his transfer, Kramer was killed while working undercover in a buy-bust investigation.

Conclusion

The Successful Spy

You will never read about successful spies in the newspaper or watch them being interviewed on TV talk shows. Only failure makes a spy famous. Success guarantees that the public will never know the spy's name—and neither will the victims who suffered the results of his efforts.

Around the world, every day, thousands of men and women go to work planning to steal the most valued thing with which they are entrusted: the secrets of their employers, fellow citizens, and friends. Their victims often believe these traitors to be exemplary employees, loyal confederates, and faithful friends. Most of the time, the traitors will spy for years, even decades, without ever being discovered or even suspected.

The vast majority of those who become successful spies never planned or expected to become traitors. They took the jobs that positioned them so that they had access to valuable secrets, expecting to work their careers out as loyal and honest employees. Many will even deny the accusation of treason, insisting that they were forced to take the only course of action possible because others betrayed them, took advantage of them, or denied them a fair shake in life. Even those who admit that they have turned traitor will offer complicated excuses for why their actions are justified.

The case officers who turned them into traitors knew how to help them find that justification. Behind every successful spy is a successful intelligence case officer who deliberately conned the person into becoming a spy. Good case officers never see their names in the newspaper either.

Yet, the key to spying success is not the spy or the case officer who recruits the spy. In the final analysis, every successful spy owes his success to the person upon whom he is spying. Just like thieves thrive when people are careless with how they protect their valuables, so, too, do spies thrive when people are careless with the way they protect their secrets.

Most readers will never have any reason to recruit a spy. Intelligent, strong, self-reliant, courageous, and competent people don't have to steal secrets to survive and prosper while defending themselves from aggressors. If you have an enemy on the border, the way to make sure he never attacks is not to steal his plan of attack. Instead, you must arm and prepare to defeat any attack that the aggressor might launch and then let him know exactly how strong you are. If you don't prepare that kind of defense, then stealing every one of your enemy's secrets won't save you from disaster.

If a business competitor is outperforming you, the answer is not to steal his secrets; it's to better serve your customers and keep them coming back. If you want to beat a political opponent, the answer is not waging dirty tricks, lying campaigns, or hiring petty criminals to break into your rival's office; it's taking a logical stance on issues, offering simple explanations, good advertising, and the courage to be honest with the voters. If you have a personal relationship with a lover or a partner that has degenerated to the point that you must spy on that person—or worse, you fear that he may be spying on you—it has already failed and the best thing you can do is end it as quickly as possible.

The paradox is that the more competent, clever, and successful you become in business, social relations, government, politics, or your personal life, the more likely it is that someone will set out to steal your secrets of success and use that information to destroy you. If you are really good at what you do, your enemy will not succeed in defeating you, even if he succeeds in stealing your secrets. More likely, you won't have any secrets worth stealing. The strongest, most successful people in the world live their lives as open books, caring not a whit about keeping secrets. Indeed, they want the world to know how strong they are.

However, many of you may not have that strength of character, and you do have secrets you think you need to keep. If your enemies succeed in learning what you want to keep hidden from the world, their successful spying will cost you money, pain, worry, frustration, and even defeat. It is for you that this book is really written. The more you know about how spies are recruited, the better prepared you will be to recognize the spies within your own ranks and neutralize them or even turn them against the people who recruited them.

The person who successfully spies on you will not be some funny-looking stranger or someone who openly challenges your authority or makes his dislike for you obvious. The person who spies on you will be someone you trust. It may be your secretary, your most faithful employee, your good friend, or even your lover.

If you have a traitor in your midst, the thing you must understand is that something went wrong long before the spy master came along and convinced that person to betray you. Good case officers must have human material to work with. The best way to protect against the spy is to make sure that the only people who have access to your secrets are people who have as much to gain by keeping those secrets as you do.

Whether you are running a country, a business, a criminal enterprise, or a political movement, or just living well on your own hard work, here are a few things you can do to make sure someone you trust doesn't listen to the siren call of treason.

- *Never accept people based on what they, or others, say they are.* Find out what they have done. Whether you are hiring an employee, accepting volunteer help in a political action group, or starting a friendship or a love affair, thoroughly check out the background of everyone you must trust. The things that count are not letters of recommendation, the praises of peers, or the fawning adulation of their friends, but credit records, school records, court and criminal records (or, better said, the lack of such records), and past successes or failures in sports, business, employment, and personal living.
- *Past behavior is no guarantee of future behavior.* No matter how sterling someone's background or past work performance, watch for evidence that doesn't track with what you already know. Decide based on what people do today, not what they did yesterday, and certainly never what they say they will do tomorrow.
- *Do not rely on quick fixes such as polygraph examinations, scheduled security clearance updates, surprise audits, surveillance cameras, or electronic eavesdropping as a means of revealing spies.*
- *Be security conscious and educate those you trust on how intelligence case officers recruit spies.* Offer substantial rewards for anyone who reports a possible approach by an enemy espionage officer.
- *Don't identify your own counterespionage officers.* (You don't have a counterespionage officer? If you keep valuable secrets, you want someone on the payroll whose job it is to guard those secrets.) Don't put those charged with counterespionage in the security office that looks after the physical and personal security of the building and the employees. Counterespionage officers should work under cover as personnel officers, special assistants, legal aids, morale officers, or any other title that allows them to move easily among your employees and gather information without anyone suspecting what they are really doing.

- *Learn as much about your employees who have access to your secrets as any enemy case officer could learn.* Your counterespionage officers should look at every employee with access to secrets on a regular (but random) basis by using the same techniques that a recruiting case officer would use. That means secret surveillance that neither the employee nor anyone except you and the counterespionage officer knows is going on. (Sure, that's expensive, but if the CIA had been doing that instead of trusting in lie detectors, Rick Ames would have been caught in the first year he started spending the extra money he earned by spying for the KGB.)
- *Don't keep things secret that don't have to be kept secret.* Know what is vital intelligence that must be protected and restrict access to such information only to those who need to know.
- *Develop sound personnel practices that reward effort, creativity, and loyalty.* Make sure they reach down to the little people who are such an attractive target for spy recruiters. Anyone with access to secret material or areas where secret material is held should be paid extra money for the trust you place in them. Secretaries who type up secret documents should make as much as college-educated company executives and should be treated with the same respect.
- *Don't keep disgruntled employees on the payroll, especially employees who feel they haven't been treated fairly.* If you can't promote the man who thinks he deserves a promotion, fire him. Don't leave him in place.
- *Don't keep any employee in a position that gives him access to secrets if he develops any vices or habits such as alcohol or drug abuse, credit problems, dangerous or offensive sexual behavior, or personality disorders.* (This flies in the face of the modern idea of vice as a disease, but tolerance for bad behavior is one of the primary reasons why American intelligence agencies lost the spy war.)
- *Be tolerant of unusual or different behavior that does not impact*

on job performance or the employee's personal relations. Don't fire the open homosexual who lives quietly with a partner. Do fire the married man who cheats on his wife every chance he gets, lies to her and his colleagues about what he is doing, and uses his work as a cover to get away with it.

Of course, following these rules will not guarantee that no one will ever steal your secrets. But real life has no guarantees—something that every good case officer knows. He takes the human material he finds, and he manipulates it into something he can use. You can do the same, whether your are trying to recruit a spy or make sure your employees, friends, and lovers stay faithful to you.

If you liked this book, you will also want to check out these: